Barney was watching the changing eagerness on Margaret's sweet face, the look of joy in her beautiful eyes, and suddenly forgetful of the watching eyes about them, he murmured softly:

"You dear!" And then without warning, and certainly without definite intention beforehand, he stooped quickly and kissed her!

Tyndale House books by Grace Livingston Hill.
Check with your area bookstore for these best-sellers.

TIME OF THE
SINGING OF BIRDS

LIVING BOOKS ®
Tyndale House Publishers, Inc.
Wheaton, Illinois

This Tyndale House book
by Grace Livingston Hill
contains the complete text
of the original hardcover edition.
NOT ONE WORD
HAS BEEN OMITTED.

Printing History
J. B. Lippincott edition published 1944
Tyndale House edition/1991

Living Books is a registered trademark of Tyndale
House Publishers, Inc.

Library of Congress Catalog Card Number 91-65397
ISBN 0-8423-7209-1
Copyright © 1944 by Grace Livingston Hill
Cover artwork copyright © 1991 by Corbert Gauthier
All rights reserved
Printed in the United States of America

98 97 96 95 94 93 92 91
 8   7   6   5   4   3   2   1

THE birds were singing madly in the old orchard around the house when Barney Vance woke up that first morning back in the old house where he was born and brought up, and where, two years before, he had kissed his mother good-by to go across the seas and fight. Now he was Lieutenant Vance and had been invalided out of the army and sent home to recuperate, with little probability that he would be called back. His strong young body had taken a terrible beating during his last engagement with the enemy, and the doctor had thought there was grave doubt whether it would ever get back to the old vigor where he could hope to go on and continue fighting. And he had been tired. So tired! And glad to rest a bit, though in his heart of hearts he had the determination to be back on the job again as soon as he recovered his normal strength. But now he was here, and it was good to rest. It was like crawling into a foxhole when the enemy got too strenuous, and he was temporarily out of ammunition. It was good to find a real haven. That was how he had felt as he swung off the midnight train last night at the little flag station, where he knew he would have to walk over a mile, to make the old home. He was none too ready for that dark lonely walk, but it was home, and it was where he had a right to be, and he wanted to get there, so he had walked. He had stumbled up to the porch seat after sounding the knocker, and dropped down with his head leaning against the clapboards of the old house, his eyes closed.

Of course he knew that his mother was gone. Word of her death had come to him while he was still in the hospital, recovering from his desperate wounds, and had much delayed his chances of restoration to health. But he had fought that long battle out, and recognized it as one of the inevitable chances of war he had taken when he bade his mother good-by. She herself had seen it, and reminded him that she might not be there when he returned, reminded him that she would be watching for him in Heaven. He had known that she would not be in the old farmhouse to meet him. He had reminded himself of that fact again and again during the long journey. And yet he had wanted to come.

There would be nobody at the old home to meet him but the two old servants, old Joel Babbit, and his wife Roxy, who had been in charge of the house and the farm ever since he could remember. That is, he hoped they were still there. For after his mother was gone there had been no one to write to him about things but old Roxy, and she wasn't much of a correspondent. Still he had hoped. Roxy used to love him, and next to his mother would be more like homefolks than anybody he knew. And so he had kept on hoping through every hard step of that mile and a half he had walked from the station.

And Roxy had come to answer that knock. He had known she would if she was alive. And if she wasn't, what did it matter? That was how he felt as he slumped to the porch seat and waited.

And then there was her step, in the old felt bedroom slippers, down at the heel, shuffling along, a candle in her hand, to supplement the electricity that she had turned on at the head of the stairs.

Roxy had brought him in and crooned over him, called him her dear boy, and drawn him into the old front room, where she had always kept a fire laid ready for lighting should he ever return.

"I promised yer mommie, ye know," she said as she knelt and touched her candle to the kindling and whipped up a fire in no time.

Of course it wasn't cold weather, for those birds wouldn't have been singing so joyously now this morning if it were, but he remembered the fire had felt good to his stiff joints and aching muscles last night, and the crackling of the flames as they snapped the dry old twigs had sounded cheerily as if they were welcoming him, even though there were only two very humble retainers besides themselves to do it.

Those were the first impressions he had as he gradually came awake. Something cheery, in spite of the fact that it was all sad, because his mother was gone; and wouldn't be back there any more—wouldn't be there to ask him all about his experiences, nor to mourn over his wounds, nor worry lest there might be aftereffects. She had gone to another world, where wounds down here didn't matter any more. Oh, she would be sympathetic with his worries even now, up in Heaven, where he was sure she had gone! But they wouldn't pierce her own soul the way his bumps and bruises used to do even when he was just a little child and fell down on the old doorstone at the kitchen steps, and skinned his knee. He always knew those bruises of his hurt his mother even more than they did him. He came to know that at a very early age when he watched the slow tears travel down her smooth cheek as she bathed the blood away and put on the lotion, wincing herself because it smarted him. He remembered asking her then, "Does it hurt your fingers when you put it on my cut?" And she had smiled and shaken away the tears, and said, "No, it doesn't hurt mother."

"Then why does you cwy?" And she had answered tenderly, "Oh, I guess I was feeling how it hurt you, little boy. That's what made the tears come. I don't like anything to hurt my brave boy."

He remembered puzzling over that, and then asking, "Is I your brave boy, muvver?"

She had looked at the lingering tears on his cheeks, and then smiled a bit sadly, "Well, perhaps not just yet, dear. But you're *going* to be brave by-and-by. Brave people don't cry for hurts you know. They bear a hurt quietly, with beautiful courage. When you grow up you will grow courageous I hope."

He could remember every word she had said about being brave. Dear mother! He remembered her tender smile. Somehow it almost comforted him for her absence now. It was the greatest hurt he had, that she was gone. Was he being brave about it? And would she think, was she thinking now, where she was in Heaven; was she feeling satisfied that he had been brave in the war he had been fighting? There was a time to which he could look back, when his very soul had been torn with pain, and he had remembered her words then, of how a real man would be brave, even when suffering great pain.

Over on the other side of the room lay his uniform, a purple heart and a silver star adorned its somberness, but what were they to him now? Would his mother think he had won the silver star? Would she have been pleased?

Oh, yes, she would! But he must not think about that now. He had come home and she was not here. He had a new life to live, though he had little heart for it, now, when it suddenly dawned upon him that he was here. Here in the old house, where he had so longed to be! Here with the old apple trees around him in full bloom, and the birds singing their tumultuous songs, just as if there had been no war. Just as if there were no death, and no more war going on even now, where some of his former comrades were going bravely into fire. Birds singing. Almost as if it might be Heaven and he was hovering on the edge of it, as if there were no sorrow, and only peace and joy. Glad birds! How *could* they? How could they sing when there was still sorrow in the world?

But this couldn't last forever, this wrenching of hearts, and pain in the midst of joy. Someday there would dawn glory, and joy forever, and he must live for that time. It sounded almost like a sermon he was preaching to himself these first dawning thoughts of home coming.

But there were sweet things to think about too. Perhaps they were some of the themes of the songs those little birds were singing out there among the apple blossoms.

And there had been old Roxy, coming to the door to let him in, her old arms about him, a tenderness in their touch that reminded him of his mother's touch. She had been his nurse and comforter long ago while his mother was still there. Now she would go on comforting him, just with a gentle hand, the kindliness in her voice, the look in her old eyes, the good things with which she would feed him.

Even last night she had brought him hot broth, and fed him as if he had been that little child she had loved from his babyhood. He had been so tired, and so nearly overcome with exhaustion from his long walk after weeks in the hospital, that he had scarcely thanked her. It had been good to him to be fed. Then she had called old Joel, and together they had got him upstairs to his old room, with the sweet-smelling sheets fresh from their hiding among lavender blossoms, the cool pillows under his head with their breath of lavender. How homelike it had all been, as if his mother had ordered it for him, as if she had arranged it and left it ready when she had to go off to Heaven!

So he lay and came slowly back to waking again on a new day. A day where he must be brave. Even though he bitterly missed the past, he must be brave.

He must stop this kind of reminiscing. It was glooming the first morning of his day at home. He must not let that be. What was it he had anticipated so keenly, beyond the mere getting here and feeling the old home about him? He had known his mother was gone, and yet he had wanted to come. What else was there in the life he had left behind those two long years ago?

Friends? Yes, there were a lot of friends of course. But the fellows were all off in the service somewhere. Two who had been very close, he had left lying on the battlefield that last night he was in action and was carried off himself, waking up in a hospital a long time afterward. Girls? Yes, there had been girls, a lot of attractive ones, but he hadn't wanted to marry any one of them. He had been very young when he went away to college. He hadn't begun to think about marrying yet. Some of them had been rather sweet. One he had heard was married now, and another had died in an accident. But there had been others. Where were they now? Probably off doing war nursing, or working in some war plant, though he didn't know of such a place in this vicinity. There might be, of course. He would presently have to look up some of those old contacts. They would have changed some with the years, probably, and world happenings. He must have changed, too. But it would be pleasant to get together with someone he used to know and talk over old times, find out what had become of this one and that one of whom he had lost track.

There had been Hank Bristow and Casper Withrow. They were probably in the war somewhere. Maybe someone knew. He must get Roxy to talking. She would have heard. Roxy never used to miss a trick in the old days, and she loved to talk when she was in the mood.

There had been Hortense Revenal. What had become of her? She and her mother had come to board over at the next farm a couple of summers before the war. She had been in high school with him, and much in evidence at all the school parties and activities. And because of their living in the same neighborhood it had often fallen to his lot to see her home from gatherings. As she grew older she developed a possessiveness that had not pleased his mother. What was it about her that mother had criticized? She said she was bold and was much too sophisticated for her age. This was after Hortense had returned from a summer with her father, who was estranged from his wife, and lived in New York. It was rumored there was a divorce in the offing. Hortense's mother was a giddy person who paid very little attention to her child, and had many week-end visitors from a distance. His own mother used always to have a troubled look in her eyes whenever Hortense had been much in his company.

But it had been no wonder that Hortense was often coming over to see him on one pretense or another, a problem she could not solve, or a Latin sentence she could not translate, and then would stay for a few games.

Poor kid! She had nothing at home to attract her. He had felt sorry for her. And mother had been very kind to her of course. She would always bring her sewing and sit in the room, sometimes playing games with them, taking part in their talk, occasionally reading aloud to them. But he had a strong feeling that his mother had been much relieved when Hortense went to visit her father, or went away to see her grandmother or one of her aunts. His mother definitely had objected to Hortense. Well now, why? That was a question he would have to take out and examine and sift, in case Hortense should turn up again. Just why hadn't mother felt easy in having her come over so often? It couldn't be just that mother was old-fashioned and didn't like the way Hortense was dressed, too elaborately, or something of that sort.

Hortense had large appealing black eyes, a dominating personality, and a way of ignoring questions of right and wrong, truth and falsehood, mine and thine. He could look back and see that now. Was it just because his mother had called his attention to it or had he known it all the time and had he excused it because Hortense had a sort of personal fascination for him?

Well, she had been only a kid then, and he hadn't been much more himself. If mother were here now she might not have the same objection, and of course his mother wouldn't want him to be biased by her judgments of several years ago. Still, he was not deeply anxious to see Hortense. If she came in his way well and good. If not, well, that was that. It was only childhood stuff, anyway. Of course if he found she was still living in the old place he would have to go and call, after awhile, when he got strong enough to feel like visiting. Then he could judge if he wanted to see her any more. He could ask Roxy about her. But of course Roxy had never liked her either.

And there had been Lucy Anne Salter, and the Wrexall twins, Madge and Martha, and Janet Harper. But hadn't he heard that Janet had gone overseas, in some capacity, a WAC or a WAVE or one of those things? He wasn't sure. Somehow in those two terrible years of his absence the things he had left behind had grown so unimportant. Well, perhaps it wouldn't have been that way if his mother had lived and kept on writing her wonderful letters to him. How he used to envy the other fellows after she was gone when they got a letter from their mothers! Well, there! He must stop that. That kind of a memory would bring smarting tears to his eyes, and a soldier did not wear tears. Even if he had been in bed for weeks and weeks, and was all unnerved. He must brace up. Listen to those birds. They were screaming their joy of the morning, and he must be glad too, for he was at home, where he had wanted for so long to be. He was here, and the morning sounded good, and the breath of apple blossoms was borne on the soft April air. "The time of the singing of birds" had come. He had liked that verse when he was a kid.

But home without mother wasn't all he had hoped it would be. Out there in a foreign land in a hospital, home had seemed just Heaven, even with his mother gone. Her presence would sort of be lingering around. And it was. Yes, he could remember when she would come into the room in the morning and pull his shades down, to let him sleep a little longer. But there! He mustn't remember. It would get him all stirred up.

It was early yet, and he was still weary. He would just turn over and go to sleep again.

So the birds sang on and lulled him into a dream of his mother, who seemed to come and soothe his forehead, and tell him to lie still and rest yet a little while, as she used to do. And so he slept again.

2

THE journey home had been precarious, and wearisome. There were so many changes, and he scarcely got over the excitement of one stage of it until another was thrust upon him. Change of scene, conditions, environment, and personnel of his companions.

From the first suggestion of it, the doctor and the nurses had been opposed to letting him go. They felt it was too soon to move him. He had so recently been considered one who would not recover from that last terrible engagement.

"It's all wrong," said the doctor. "Lieutenant Vance should not be moved for at least another month. If they insist upon it I will not answer for the consequences. He is too valuable a man to be taking any chances with his life."

"Yes, I agree with you," said Barney Vance's captain. "He is too valuable a man."

But when they asked Barney himself they found him strangely indifferent—just that pleasant grin, and a quiet lifting of his eyebrows.

"It's all right with me, Doc," he said. "It feels good to rest for awhile."

The eyes of the doctor and the captain met with that negative glance that was decisive.

"He doesn't seem to care," said the puzzled captain, back in the shack he called his headquarters. "I thought he'd be all on fire to get home."

A waiting private looked up, saluted respectfully, and said:

"Beg pardon, sir, but perhaps you don't know that guy just recently received word from home that his mother's dead. He wouldn't be so keen about anything just now. He banked a lot on his mother."

"Oh," said the captain, "I didn't know! How unfortunate he should have got the message yet. He is in no state of health to bear any more shocks. They should have had a care how they gave him letters."

"Oh, he's taking it all right! He's that kind of a guy!"

"Yes, I know," said the captain, "he would. A fellow who could do what he's just got done doing to the enemy, and manage to get back alive, and *live,* wouldn't fall down on any of the other attacks of life. He's *real,* that man!"

The young private's eyes were filled with agreement.

"He sure is!" he answered, lifting a look like the raising of a banner.

But definitely, the idea of sending Barney Vance home on furlough was postponed.

Then suddenly an order came through to evacuate the position, abandon the hospital, and equipment, except such as could be gathered in haste, and depart. Warning had come that the enemy was on the way.

By night, in a shackly old ambulance they hastily bundled Barney Vance over rough roads, or no roads at all. They jolted frightfully, bringing all the pain of the past weeks back into the weakened body that had been bearing so much—bumping into looming trees in the pathway, not even stars to light them. There was distant booming of enemy fire, frightening rumors brought by stealthy scouts, whispered orders, hurrying feet, muted motors, and then an open sky. Careful, anxious hands carried the patients hurriedly across a stubbly field, and deposited them in haste in an airplane. A jerk, a roar, a dash, and they were soaring up, somehow like the eventualities of battle that had been so much a part of his life and thoughts for the past months, that he was plunged backward and roused to a tense alertness, wondering if he was responsible again to help quell what was going on. Then the whir of wings overhead, around, everywhere! Was the enemy pursuing? He looked up with a strange apathy, as he felt that they were mounting. Would they escape? Or was this the end, in a decrepit airplane, unable to escape? Shot down at the last, ignominiously, after two years of noble fighting! At least they all called the work he had done noble. But there didn't seem much nobility to an end like this. Crippled, weak, sick, and no chance for escape!

Still they were mounting. Were they going up to God now? Well the enemy wouldn't come that far, at least. Enemies would have to stop before they reached God's throne. That was one refuge they would not dare to face.

He drew a weary relaxed breath as he felt their altitude. Clouds about, below! He raised up on one elbow to get a glimpse out the window. There didn't seem to be an enemy in sight. Had they lost them? But there was still the sound of bombs far below. Would the clouds keep their secret, or part and give the enemy another view to follow?

He dropped wearily back on the roughly improvised pillow and closed his eyes. What did it matter? He *had* to go to sleep. Even in such straits, he *had* to go to sleep.

When he awoke it was night, and they were coming

down silently in the darkness. There was some trouble about refueling, but it didn't have to concern him, though he was comfortably relieved when he felt the lift of wings again. They were going high now, but he did not look out to see if they were followed. He did not care. Perhaps they were really going to God, and that was all right with him if they did. He knew God. He had got acquainted with Him out there on the battlefield in all that stress. Of course his mother had tried to teach him from the time he was a mere babe, but it hadn't somehow meant anything to him till he got out there facing danger. Danger and a battlefield. That was a great place to have God, the great God, come walking toward you with welcome on His face. A hand held out to help and lift. No, he wasn't afraid of God.

When he woke again he was being carried on a stretcher to a dim building where was a hospital of sorts. But it didn't matter. He was glad of any anchorage for the time.

There followed an indeterminate period of dullness. Waiting for orders. Waiting for transportation. And then more journeyings. A ship at last. But it was all hazy. He hadn't even then quite aroused to the consciousness of the moment enough to ask just where in the great world he was, or perhaps no one talked about those things. He hadn't entirely come out of the stress of war far enough to care much. There were only two places that mattered any more. Where he was, and home. And perhaps home was only a great wistfulness now, since he had had the word that his mother was gone. It was all just a great weariness, and wanting to get where he might have the say of what he should do and when he should eat and sleep. Rest was a great need.

Then the rough truck-journey to the ship, his first attempts to walk about by himself, without much desire to do so. Was it always going to be like this? This great aversion of his body to take the initiative in any movement? Would this continue? Was he half dead already? He wasn't afraid of death outright, but this deadness of senses, this apathy of mind, this terrible weakness, it was intolerable. Sinking into a deck chair and closing his eyes brought momentary relief. Gradually the quiet of the sea, the invigorating salt air, cleared his brain. Hours came when he could walk with almost a spring in his step, when he could look off over the blue of the sea. Such peace of blue with sunlight on its billows. So wide, so quiet, so far from tumult and war! He was sailing, sailing! It was better than sailing up among the clouds. It was quieter. It rested him. This might go on forever.

In the night the scene of peace changed. An ominous sound. Was it wind? Or wings? Motors? Hurrying footsteps, voices, shouts, sudden lights, startling words hurled hissingly through long whispers. And again the old tumult back, a pounding heart, presaging disaster. The enemy again? He must get up and fight for victory. He could not lie here and rest when the enemy was rampant again.

Explosions! Yes, that must be a submarine! He sprang from his berth to investigate. A sudden long shudder through the ship. More explosions! He shook the sleep from his eyes and tried to think. He was back on the alert again now, dropping into the old training, thinking quickly, working fast, back among the crew taking a hand, his weakness forgotten, his mind racing ahead. Long hours of activity, anxiety, readiness for what might come, no time to think of where he was going, nor how it was going to be when he got there. No time to rest, or even to sleep or eat. No one with time enough to prepare meals. Putting out fires, saving their ship. There was plenty to be done, and not even a doctor with time enough to notice whether he was fit for the work he was doing.

He told himself that perhaps it was as well, that is, when he had a split second to think about it. He had been getting lazy. That apathy was gone. It took an enemy, and threat of disaster, to bring him back to normal again. Oh, perhaps there might be a reaction afterwards, and the apathy return. What he was doing now might retard his final recovery. Oh, well, what matter? This was the job at hand and it must be done. Something that future generations might need for their well-being. This was what he was set to do. His business in life was to help win the war, not to humor his physical needs.

So, the hours went by, and the ship was saved, the submarine vanquished. The anxiety lessened and a great impatience followed, a gradual lethargy stealing on again, as native skies drew nearer. Strange ships dimly on the horizon, airplanes at night! Would they never reach the land, the place of peace?

He had thought when he left his home that he would not return until every enemy was vanquished, yet here he was, almost at home, and the war not won yet! A rising shame engloomed him. What had he not done that he might have done to save his world? He had wrought his best, and here he was almost back among a people that had expected so much of him and his companions, and now they had had to send him home, without them. It was ridiculous. He went over there to *die,* didn't he? Why didn't they let him stay and die then? He could have sent a *few* more deadly shots, couldn't he, before he was done? What matter if he died doing it, after he had done his best? Why hold him to recover? Just his few last shots might have helped the deciding battle.

Those were his last thoughts before he dropped out of consciousness.

The birds sang on. And off in the distance there came the sound of a cooing dove, bringing dimly to mind the rest of that verse. "The time of the singing of birds is come, and the voice of the turtle (dove) is heard in our land."

3

THREE boys were wheeling by the old Vance house on bicycles that rattled and clattered, and showed their age gaily and nonchalantly. They looked toward the old house with something of a possessiveness in their eyes.

"What's become of the guy that usedta live here?" asked Jimmy Holzer. "He get killed er somepin'?"

"Naw," said Billy Lang, "I heard it was worse'n that. I guess he got took prisoner, by the Japs, I guess it was, ur else the other fellas."

"Naw! You're wrong!" said Boog Tiller importantly. "He got took by the Japs, all righty, after he'd brought down seventeen of those mosquito things, ur mebbe it was twenty-six, I ferget which. An' then they got him, and tuk him to n'nterment camp, I guess it was, but he escaped, see? And he had all kinds of a time gettin' back to his outfit, an' mos' died on the way, only some pal of his found him and carried him back to his own company, an' he's been in the hospital an awful long time. He was hurt bad, y'know. But they say now he's gonta get well after all, an' he's gonta be sent home fer rest, sometime, mebbe soon."

"You mean he's gonta come back here to Vance's Point? You mean we can see him again sometime, Boog?"

"Could be," said Boog, speculatively.

"Oh, gee! Wouldn't that be great? Mebbe they'll have a celebration with a procession an' eats an' things, an' we can be there!"

"Could be," said Boog again, contemplating the possibility of giving out such information as a fact, and whether it might have any bad reactions for the giver of such news, provided it didn't turn out to be exactly true. However, one could always qualify it by prefacing such information by the words: "I heard—"

But the subject of all this speculation was sweetly sleeping behind the apple blossom screen, and didn't hear. Even though the voices of the boys were by no means hushed, but rang out clearly as if they wanted to make an audience hear. So they wheeled on around the bend of the road, and could be heard no more.

Two old men and their hired helper sitting in the back of a truck steadying a plow, were the next to pass by.

"I see that young Vance has been doing great things over there across the water," said Ezekiel Summers, as he drove down the road gripping the wheel of his car with his gnarled old hands, and nodding toward the old house. "Pity his ma ain't alive to know about it. They tell me where they read in the papers how he got a star and a purple something for honorable bravery—ain't that what they call it? Yes, it certainly is a pity his ma can't know about it. It would have done her heart good. She certainly did think a heap of that boy o' hers, an' rightly too. She done a good job, bringing him up, all alone as it were, without any dad ta he'p. He ain't no sis, neither, even ef he has got a collidge eddication, an' wasted a lotta time playin' ball, an' got his picter in the papers. But I guess we can rightly be proud of him in our town in spite of all that, after all them enemy planes he done for."

"Yeah," said the tough young plowman, Sam Gillers, "but they do say he's been wounded bad. Some say he may not get well. He might not even come home at all. There's thousands of them boys just die, and their folks don't know fer a long time."

"Aw, yes, their folks get notices," said Ike Peterson. "The Gov'n'ment's been real nice about sendin' their folks word about what's happened to 'em, afore they tell it to the papers, Zeke!"

"Well, yes, I guess they hev been kinda careful about sech things," said Zeke. "But you know it ain't sa easy to attend ta all sech little trifles when you've got a hull army ta look out fer. B'sides, they don't waste many words tellin' their folks. There was the Barrowses only just got word their Joe was missin' in action, an' got tuk pris'ner an' they haven't hed one word since, an' that was two years, lackin' a month, ago, an' Miz Barrows she's pretty near went crazy about that boy of hers. They oughtn't ta wait that long, I don't think."

"Well, in this case," spoke up the young plowman, "thur ain't nobody ta let know, sence Miz Vance passed on. There ain't none of his folks left around here."

"Wal, I guess Roxy an' Joel think a lot o' that Barney fella. Roxy's took care o' him sence he was a babe in arms," said Summers.

"Yes, I guess she has," said Peterson.

Their echoing voices clanged among the apple blooms and seemed to hit the very clapboards of the old house as they passed, but they did not reach the sleeper whose dreams were sweet and deep.

A little later, when the morning sun was mounting

higher, a smart car drove by with two dashing girls talking hilariously above their motor's noise.

"Oh, *Boy!* I wish this war would end!" yawned one daintily. "I'm fed up with all the things we do these days, and all the things we can't do. It's too ridiculous, telling us we can't have things we like to eat, and not giving us all the gas we want. Why I've heard there's *plenty* of gas, stored up somewhere. What right have they got to tell us we can't take pleasure rides I'd like to know? Look at all their spending, sending tanks around the world. That must cost a lot! I don't really think I believe in war, anyway," said Irma Watts. "They act like they were playing a game trying to see which could kill the most. For my part, I don't see why the good people have to go out and endanger their lives just because some crazy people over the ocean want to fight. Look at Mary Forbes having to go to work, and let her young husband go off for no telling how long, and maybe never come back. And Janet Waters with three babies to take care of. And her husband has to get called. He goes next Monday. I don't think it's fair, do you, Hortense? I don't see why somebody doesn't do something about it. I think it's time for this war to be over, don't you?"

"Yes," yawned Hortense, "I think it's an awful *bore!*"

"Say, Hortense, isn't this the old Vance house? Didn't you used to have a crush on the handsome boy they called Barney? Seems to me they told me that when I got back from visiting my grandmother. What became of him?"

"Oh, he's gone to war of course, like everybody else," said Hortense. "There's hardly any men left in town worth speaking about. But they say some of them are coming back on furloughs pretty soon. I shouldn't wonder if Barney Vance would be coming home. Nobody seems to know. Yes, I used to go with him a lot. We were practically engaged before he went to war, but of course he was pretty much under his mother's thumb, and she had a terrible religious complex. She didn't want him to do this and that, and he had to go with her to church. Even after he grew up she hung onto him, and she and I never would have hit it off. But now, she's out of the way, I might be interested in him again. We'll see! He was a nice kid, and awfully handsome of course."

"He's mebbe changed a lot himself," said Irma.

"Well, yes, probably. He wouldn't have stood for lipstick and rouge, not in the old days. But he's likely come in touch with a little European sophistication, and learned how girls ought to look. Anyhow, why should I care? If I want him I'll risk but what I can get him back, especially now that his mother is gone," and Hortense tossed her dark curls back from her forehead, and tilted her ridiculous little trifle of a hat down over one eye with anticipatory assurance, while her laugh rang out noisily and started a wood robin that was practicing a love song on a tree by Barney's window. Perhaps it was the cessation of that love song that made Barney wake up, and then the next sound that he heard was the shuffling of Roxy's old felt slippers as she scuffed along the hall that led to his room. The footsteps paused, and there came the subdued tinkle of glass against silver. Roxy was bringing his breakfast, the way she used to bring it when he was a kid and had been sick for a few days, measles or mumps or something. He half smiled and opened his eyes. Softly he heard the doorknob turn, and Roxy's gray head and the gleam of her steel-rimmed spectacles appeared cautiously.

"Hello Roxy!" he called with his old grin. "Top of the morning to you! What are you stealing in so carefully for? I don't have to go to school this morning, do I?"

Roxy almost cried at the familiar greeting, and her

sweet old lips parted in her well-remembered merry smile.

"Bless you, dear boy!" she said. "No, you don't have to go to school any more. Leastways, not to the old village school. Mayhap you'll find a few more lessons in the school of life for you to learn yet, but this morning you're home, and you have the whole day before you. Ready for breakfast, are you?"

"You betcher life, Roxy. Real home breakfast! That's something I haven't had for two long years. Whatcha got, Roxy? Is that bacon I smell? And eggs? Pancakes? Oh, *Boy!* Honey? From our bees? Say, Roxy! That's swell! I was afraid honey might be rationed, or perhaps the bees had gone to war."

Roxy laughed happily.

"No, the bees ain't gone yet. They're using mosquitoes instead in the war, I heard. I read something about that in the papers."

Roxy twinkled one of her amusing winks, and the young soldier laughed aloud, a good old-fashioned boy-laugh that greatly cheered the heart of the old nurse.

"Say, Roxy, you still have your fine old sense of humor, haven't you? That's good. You said you were getting old, Roxy, but you're mistaken. You couldn't twinkle like that if you were old."

"Oh, go way with you, child!" said Roxy happily.

"Say, this is a swell breakfast, Roxy, and I see you've started in to spoil me just the way you always did. Didn't you know I've graduated from having my breakfast in bed? They wouldn't have let me come home if I hadn't. You can't baby a big soldier like that, Roxy. The government will get after you if you do."

Roxy dropped into a straight chair with her arm over the back and sat there beaming on her adored nursling as he ate his breakfast and joked with her, till she was convinced that he had not lost any of his old spirit by going to war, grim as it must have been. And when he had eaten the last crumb she arose to take the tray.

"Want some more of anything?" she asked anxiously.

"Not on your life, Roxy," he said with a grin. "You know it doesn't do to feed a starving person too much at the first meal, and I'm sure I've already eaten twice as much as I should have eaten for the first meal at home. Now, Roxy, sit down again and tell me all about everybody. Where are all the fellows and the girls I used to run around with? Are any of them here yet?"

Roxy sighed.

"Well, no, only a couple of them. Cy Baxter is still in the bank. You know he has flat feet, and he's tried several things and they won't take him. Of course his mother's glad, but she keeps it to herself, though you can't blame her. She's almost blind, and he's all she's got."

"No, I suppose war is hard for mothers. It must have been hard for mine, although she urged me to go, said she was glad I wanted to. She always taught me to be loyal to my country, and brave to do the right thing, even if it meant fighting and dying, for a principle."

"Yes, that she would, lad. Your mother was a brave lady to the end, and I thank the Lord she didn't have to suffer too long. She was always so quiet and so brave. And she was that pleased when the piece came out in the paper saying how brave her boy was. She held the paper in her hand all that first day. She wouldn't let it go out of her sight, and she read it over till she knew it by heart. And then she'd say, 'Roxy, I knew he'd be like that. I knew he'd be brave, because his father was. I used to tell him about his father in the last war, and I knew he'd be like that! I'm glad I lived long enough to know that; though if I hadn't, doubtless my Lord would have told me about it after I get Home.'"

There were tears dropping down the boy's face before she was done.

"Oh, Roxy, I'm glad you told me that!" he said. "I'm glad she lived to know about the nice things they said. But oh, if she could have lived a little longer till I got home!"

"Yes, I know, laddie!" soothed the old woman, coming over beside the bed.

The young man had buried his face in the pillow, and his shoulders were shaking with dry soundless sobs. Only the back of his head was visible, and one arm, with his hand gripping the bedclothes. Then old Roxy bent over and patted the thick dark hair that curled over his handsome head.

"But she said for you not to grieve, you know, laddie," continued the sweet old voice. "She said for you to live out your life and be happy till it was time for you to come Home, and she'd be waiting there to welcome you."

The shaking shoulders were suddenly still, and presently the soldier turned over and brushed the tears away, with a semblance of his old grin.

"Yes, I know," he said. "Now, let's go on from here. We'll talk about mother again, sometime, but now, tell me about the rest of the boys. What became of the Nezbit twins, Dave and Donnie? And where did they finally get away to? And where is Will Glegg?"

"Well, let me see. Dave an' Donnie, why they're over in Iceland, and homesick as they can be fer a sight of home. Donnie wrote back last fall some other fella got an autumn leaf in a letter from a girl, an' it made them all envious, wantin' ta get back. An' Willy Glegg, he's somewheres in Africa. They certainly do think up the most heathenish places to send our boys to, seem's if they might have gone where they wouldn't have to learn a new language."

The forlorn soldier began to laugh, and Roxy was pleased, and rattled on.

"Then there was Gene Tolland, he got hisself a nice fat office job with plenty of gold stripes he hadn't earned fighting. Came back here and strutted around like he owned the earth. And Phelps Larue was missing in action. He would be, you know. He was always everywhere when he was needed, and he had plenty honors to his credit. And Taffy Rolland is out somewhere underseas in a submarine. That don't seem right either, nice quiet boy like Taffy, never did anybody any harm, and hasta go off under*sea?* How could he ever expect to do anything for the war undersea? And Bill Brower, he got killed at Guadalcanal they say, and that's about all the boys."

"And the girls?" asked the soldier. "Are they doing anything?"

"I should say they are," said Roxy. "Arta Perry and Franny Forsythe went in training for nurses. They're off on a big transport somewhere. And Betty Price is a WAC, and the Bowman girls and Lula Fritz are WAVES, or some of the A.B.C.'s, I forget what. And the Grady, and Baker, and Watson girls went into a defense plant and are welders. I must say I'm not sure I like nice girls going around doing men's work, but I suppose that's what war is, and we can't help it. Though in my day it wouldn't have been considered nice."

The young man on the bed laughed, and then after a moment he asked:

"And whatever became of Hortense? Is she around here anywhere?"

"Oh, she got herself married soon after you left," announced Roxy triumphantly.

"Married?" There was a shade of surprise in the voice of the soldier. Then after an instant, "Who did she marry?"

"Oh, she married some rich good-looking lieutenant, and then when he got himself sent away off somewhere she tried to insist he refuse to go, and when he wouldn't do as she wanted she got herself divorced. Oh, she had some other trumped up excuse, but when it came to alimony they found he wasn't so rich after all, and she sort of lost out! And now I understand she's trotting around to camps and the places they call 'Centers,' entertaining soldiers. Though it never struck me she was very entertaining. Kind of coarse and loud I thought she was."

"You never liked Hortense, did you Roxy?"

"Oh, I wasn't so keen on her of course, but I did own she used to be pretty after a fashion. But she's changed a lot. She's all painted up fit to kill, got a mouth as big as a hollyhock, all greasy red stuff. I don't know why they paint 'em so thick, if they must paint 'em. But anyhow she's a sight. However, she's got plenty fellas to run after her where she is now, though I don't know what good it'll do her, when they're all going overseas all the time."

"No, you never did like Hortense," laughed the young man. "I always knew that."

"Well, neither did your mother," said Roxy belligerently, looking grim and sober. "Say, would you like another batch of pancakes? The griddle is still on. It won't take a minute."

"No, oh, no! I've eaten a big breakfast already, and I ought to be getting up sometime pretty soon."

"Oh, why not lie still and get a good rest? You had a long journey and you need to really sleep a lot to make up your strength. There won't be anybody around today. They don't know you're home yet, you know.

You just keep quiet a day or two, till you really feel like going out. I won't let on you've come till you're ready to see people, and I'll tell Joel to keep mum too."

"All right," grinned the soldier, "maybe I will. This bed still feels pretty good to me," and he turned over and settled down for another nap.

Then out in the hall he heard the telephone ring, and heard the felt slippers shuffle to answer it. His senses were already drowsy with the thought that there was no need for him to rouse yet, but he heard a raucous voice, a girl's voice, asking a question about himself.

"When is Barney coming back?" it said.

Then his senses came alive a little. That was Hortense's voice, wasn't it? Sharper, more nasal, more possessive than it used to be?

And then Roxy, disapproving, reproving, quite final: "Why, I really couldn't say!"

Barney grinned silently.

Then the other voice, murmuring sharply again. But something had happened to the telephone now. He couldn't hear the annoyed questions that were being asked next, for it seemed that Roxy's capable hand was being laid firmly over some part of the mechanism of the instrument so that the sound would not penetrate to the other end of the hall, and he could vision Roxy, standing there with her thin lips firmly set in a grim line. Then he heard Roxy's voice again: "No, I really couldn't say! No, I couldn't say!" That last with finality, and then the click of the receiver as Roxy hung up.

The young man on the pillow grinned to himself again. Foiled! Hortense was foiled, effectively. And yet apparently Roxy hadn't told any lies. Just reiterated that she couldn't say. And he knew her of old, that her grim conscience would not hold her to account for that statement, even though it was not made with the meaning that it might be understood to have. Roxy had a clever way of protecting her beloved ones when she felt they needed protection. And still grinning, the young man closed his eyes and surrendered himself to the luxury of going on with the rest he had been definitely ordered to take every day when he got home. Oh, it was good to be at home!

When next he came awake, some hours later, it was the clear sweet notes of a whistle that brought him back to his senses. It was a peculiar whistle, one that was all his own, and nobody else had ever seemed to be able to imitate, though many had tried. Its sweetness swept across his heart like a skillful hand on the strings of a harp, bringing back old days when home had been the place he loved best, and there was no grim specter of war anywhere. It was a sound of heartening cheer, and it almost seemed to him that it came out of his dreams, so sweet and perfect it had been. Not just one note, but several tones, like a bit of a message. It was that peculiar trill that was not easy to imitate. He must have dreamed it! But no, there it was again, and now he was hearing the crunch of bicycle wheels on the gravel of the drive. Someone was coming to the house, and giving that clarion call of his.

He sprang from the bed and stole to the window, peering from behind the curtain. Had some other boy succeeded in getting that whistle?

But now he could see, it was not a boy. It was a girl, riding a bicycle, carrying a small parcel in the rack before her. A girl with a cloud of golden hair.

He stepped back so he would not be seen, but kept her in view. Who could she be?

Then she called.

"Roxy! Oh, Roxy! Where are you? Mother sent you a pat of her new butter."

The girl stepped from her wheel, and lifted her face to

scan the windows of the house. She was very lovely. A flash of shy blue eyes, wide and sweet, a beautiful face framed in apple blossoms. Then he heard Roxy's voice as she opened the kitchen door, and the vision vanished. There was only the bicycle lying on its side against the grassy terrace, and the sound of the closing kitchen door. She had gone inside. Who was she?

Yet that whistle still seemed to linger on the air hauntingly. Was she someone to whom he had tried to teach it?

Then a robin came noisily back to the branch by the window, looked down at the wheel on the ground, and turned a beady, wondering eye on Barney as he stirred behind the curtain.

4

HE waited breathlessly behind the screening curtain, and presently he heard the kitchen door open again, low voices, just a few words, then the girl came out, flinging backward to Roxy a kiss from her finger tips, and the single word: "Bye!" as she mounted her wheel and rode away. Out the gravel drive, down the road, a slender graceful figure in a soft gray suit with a rosy collar, a bright blue sweater, and gold hair flying back from her shoulders. She made a picture that toned well into the background of apple blossoms and tender new leaves. Barney behind his window curtain, and the fat robin on his branch, stood and watched her as she flashed out into the sunlight and on down the road. Almost she might have been a bird, so swiftly and easily she rode.

When she disappeared from sight down toward the village the bird unfurled his wings and sailed into the spring sunshine, and the young man turned and picked up his garments to make a swift toilet. He had no desire any longer to lie and sleep. He wanted to get back into life and find out who that girl was, and how she happened to be able to give that whistle, which he had always supposed was his own private property.

Barney appeared down in the kitchen very soon.

"Roxy, wasn't there someone here a few minutes ago?" he asked, after he had greeted her. "Who was it?"

"Oh," said Roxy with distress in her tone, "did we waken you? I tried to be very quiet."

"No, you didn't waken me," laughed Barney. "It was the whistle wakened me. Roxy, who can whistle like that? I didn't know anybody but myself had that trick."

"Well, it was yourself that taught her to whistle. You've nobody else to blame."

"*I* taught her?" exclaimed the young man amazed. "But I don't remember ever teaching any of the *girls* to whistle. I didn't think they could. I tried to teach a couple of children now and then, but they couldn't seem to get it."

"Well, *one* of 'em did!" said Roxy firmly. "And it wasn't one of them silly girls that used to swarm around here, either. It was one of the little ones. Think back, boy, and see if you can't figure out who it was. You took a lot of pains teaching her, and she never forgot. She practiced and practiced after you went away, and once in a while she would come over to me and say, 'Roxy, do I sound all right now? Do I do it at all the way Barney did?' And I would tell her how it sounded to me. But she said she wouldn't be satisfied till I couldn't tell the difference. Till she could make me think it was you come back again. So one morning she came early while I was getting breakfast for Joel, and I heard her whistling, and I went quick to the door with my heart all a-twitter, for I really thought it was you, come back somehow! Yes, I did! And when I saw her pert little face all a-twinkle, I knew she had reached her ambition and she could whistle as well as you did. So—that's the story!

And to think you should hear her your first day when she didn't even know you were home!"

"Roxy, you don't mean that was Sunny Roselle? Not little Sunny! The little girl I used to play ball with?"

"The very same, Mr. Barney. She hasn't changed a mite, only grown up a little bit."

"But, I don't understand. The last time I saw her I'm sure she was only a child. Where has she been all this time? I haven't seen her since I went away to college. I thought the family had moved away. Didn't someone say so?"

"Children do grow up, you know," laughed Roxy. "And you remember there were two summers when you went out to the Warren farm to work as soon as you came back from college. You didn't see much of her then. And the next year she went off to stay with her grandmother who was getting old and sick and needed her. She was out there three years, off and on, her mother, too, part of the time, till her grandmother died, and then she came home again. No, the family didn't move away. They are right on their little farm just where they were. They still have the best garden in town, and make their own butter. Of course two of her brothers went away to the service, and there's only her youngest brother Frank left to help his father on the farm."

"Well, that's interesting," said Barney. "And I suppose Sunny is in high school by this time."

Roxy laughed.

"Yes, she's in high school all right, but she's a teacher, not a scholar. Why, boy, she must be all of nineteen by now, and they do say she's about the best teacher they ever had in that school, barring none."

"Sunny a *teacher!*" exclaimed Barney. "Why, I can't believe it. Little Sunny!"

"Wait till you see her!" said Roxy with satisfaction.

"Tell me about her," said the young man, settling back in the old kitchen chair, and clasping his hands behind his head with comfortable informality. "Is she as pretty as she used to be?"

"Prettier," said Roxy without reservation. "And she doesn't have to put a lot of paint and powder on to make herself look attractive either. She's as sweet and unspoiled as she was when she was a baby, and I don't believe you'll find another like her in the whole country round."

"Well, that's great! I've often wondered what became of her. And you say it was she who was whistling when she came in? You say I taught her to whistle like that! Well I certainly am proud to know it. That child! To think she's remembered it all these years!"

"Oh, yes, she remembered it. She never forgot anything you taught her. She adored the very ground you walked on in those days!"

"Yes we were pretty good pals," said Barney with a reminiscent grin. "But I suppose she's forgotten all about me by this time. Does she know I've come home?"

Roxy shook her head.

"No, I didn't tell her yet. I thought you wanted a few days to rest in before you began to see people."

"Oh, well, that goes for the others, but somehow I'd like to see Sunny. She's different. When will she come again?"

"Well, she's pretty busy with her school, and she helps her mother around the house too, since Miranda went down to the factory to do welding. They thought they ought to help the war that much by letting her go, and she was keen for it herself, though I guess it was hard for her to leave the Roselles, too."

"Well, then I suppose I ought to go and see Sunny, instead of expecting her to come over here the way she used to do when she was a kid," said Barney thoughtfully. "I can't make it seem real that she is grown up and rates being treated like a young woman."

"Oh, she's still a kid," smiled Roxy. "I'm sure she will be to you anyway. Yet she seldom speaks of you except to ask now and then if anything has been heard from you, and whether you're all right. She's pretty much of a lady you know. Quiet like, and eyes like two stars. She's grown up, but yes, she's still a kid," said Roxy happily. "And the sweetest kid you ever saw. She may not be fashionable, but I think she's a sight better looking than those other girls all painted up and their fingernails like birds' claws. Oh, I can't abide the way they fix their nails now!"

"Well I can't say I admire them either," said Barney with a shrug. "I wonder what they do it for? It can't be pleasant to live with clattery claws like that on their hands, and surely they're not good-looking. It gives me the shivers just to see them."

"Oh, they think it's smart!" snapped Roxy with a disapproving toss of her head. "That's all they live for nowadays, 'to be smaht!'" and she imitated a silly girl's tone so exactly that it set Barney off laughing again.

Roxy had to go out and look after her chickens then, and Barney sauntered slowly into the other part of the house. Somehow he wanted to take his first look around when he was by himself. There was something sacred in the blessed places where he remembered his mother's presence, and he wanted to take it for the first time, tenderly and alone.

Awhile he lingered in the library where she had always spent so much time. The walls were almost lined with books, dear old books that he had cherished, and his mother had loved.

Roxy, with a careful thought to Barney's tastes had

built up a delightful fire in the old fireplace, and drawn up the big chair that had always been his favorite seat, to tempt him to a pleasant rest. And it was there she found him when she came in, deep in the old chair, with a book, one of his old-time favorites, his long limbs stretched out to the pleasant warmth of the kindly blaze, comfort and peace all about him, the vague consciousness of his mother's desk there almost beside him. It seemed just as she had left it, neat papers and letters in orderly fashion, tucked into their compartments as if she had been there just that morning.

After awhile, maybe not today, but some day pretty soon, when he could bear it, he would go and sit where she had sat and look through all those papers, and perhaps read some of her last thoughts through their medium. But not now, not just this first morning. He did not want to brush aside the veil of make-believe and definitely feel that she was really gone forever—not just away. He would wait a few hours perhaps, or it might be a day or so, till he felt strong enough to stand it. But just now it was enough to sit here quietly, as if he were waiting for her to come in and talk with him. That was blessed, at least for the moment. And since he had been in the hospital he found that he had to take things of the heart slowly, adjust his mind and thoughts to the new order, and take it like a man. And that was the reason that he was so glad that Roxy was willing he should keep quietly out of sight for a little till he was used to the new way of his broken world. So he read an old book that he had loved in the past, and now and again he closed his eyes and prayed in his heart for strength to go on into the future that was before him.

His choice of course, after his resting time was done and when he felt fit again, would be to go back into war and do his part till the whole job was finished up and

Right established once more in this seething world. Till Evil was vanquished, and the world safe for everybody. But that was dependent upon how quickly his strength came back, and what the doctors said. Well, he must take it a day at a time, and be ready for whatever was planned ahead for him of course. His mother had taught him that, and his war experience had taught him too. But the waiting was not an easy thing to do when his impatient soul was daily growing more eager to be back and into the great fray again. Just to lie by, and be an invalid, that was never an easy role for Barney Vance to play.

So as he reclined in the old easy chair and tried to read a book he used to love, these thoughts drifted in a background across his mind to reassure him. This was the important thing to do first. Just let the atmosphere of home and the past saturate his weary spirit, and hearten him, before he must meet life again and go on.

Into this quiet brooding atmosphere breezed Roxy, with her kindly smile and a brimming glass of milk.

"It's time you had a sip of milk, laddie," she said, "and a cooky or two? You used to like them for a snack when you were a child."

"Oh, Roxy, you're going to spoil me completely. I can see I'll have to get away from here in a hurry or I'll not be fit to get back into war when I'm called again."

"Oh, but we'll not talk about that now," said the old nurse. "Time enough for that when the call comes. Meantime it's good to see you sit there like you used to do. The fire on one side and your mommie's desk on the other."

Roxy dropped down on a straight chair for a minute watching the soldier boy drink the milk, so evidently enjoying it.

"Have you been over to her desk?" she asked, after a minute. "I've kept it just as she left it. I thought you would enjoy going through it. Indeed I think she thought you would want to do that, too. For the very last time she was downstairs she sat at her desk working away at the bit papers, and writing a line here and there. She sat there far too long that last day, I thought, for her own good, and when I urged her to let me help her back to her bed she would shake her head, and say, 'No, Roxy, I must finish here. You know I may not be well enough to come down again perhaps, and I want to get it all in order for my boy, if he comes home after I'm gone.' So I thought you might feel it was something she left for you to go through. She might even have written a few words on something just for you, you know."

The young man caught his breath, and turned his face away toward the desk, that she might not see the mist in his eyes.

"I must go through it," he said. "I was working up to that, but I wasn't sure I was up to bearing it yet." His voice was husky and he tried to give a pitiful little grin for Roxy's sake.

Wise Roxy rose, with no sign that she saw how much he was stirred by her words, and true to her old habit of keeping cheerful in an issue, put on a matter-of-fact tone:

"That's good, of course. You don't want to get yourself all worked up. She wouldn't have wanted that. She just wanted you to be comforted. And now, don't you think you've been up long enough and you ought to get back to your bed and take another long sleep? Tomorrow or the next day will be time enough for you to look into any business papers. She said they were not important, but you would want to look them over sometime, and so she got them ready for you. Now, get you upstairs and take your nap, and after a while I'll be bringing your tray up. A bit of chicken cooked the way you used to like it. With dumplings? How is that?"

"Sounds swell," he said, slowly getting up from his chair and putting down his book on the table. "But you needn't bring it up. I can come down." Then after a minute, wistfully, "And will there be apple sauce?"

"Oh, yes, surely," said Roxy smiling and winking back a recalcitrant tear of her own.

So she shooed him off to his rest, and went out to see how the chicken was getting on, and prepare her dumplings.

Barney did not get back to the library until late the next afternoon, though the thought of that precious desk was hovering in his mind. His heart cried out to go through it at once, but he wanted to do it alone. He did not want even Roxy watching him, not even her cheery voice commenting upon whatever he might find. The contents of that desk was too sacred for others to intrude upon him while he examined it.

So he slept late, waking only to hear the morning matins of the birds among the apple blossoms, and then drifting off to sleep again, taking the real rest that the doctor had hoped he would get when he once reached home.

He came down to the kitchen while Roxy was preparing lunch and talked with her, asking about some of his mother's old friends, discovering that some had moved away and a few had died, but quite a number were still living in their old homes, and often asked after him.

There had been no sweet piercing whistle that morning to turn his thoughts toward his young friend Sunny, and perhaps a feeling of self-consciousness prevented his speaking of her again. At least she was not mentioned.

Barney ate heartily of the delightful homemade soup

compounded of meat and vegetables with plenty of light fluffy potatoes generously floating among the carrots and onions. He said how good it tasted. Told her that nobody else knew how to make soup like that, took a second helping, and then equally praised the apple and nut salad that came after, and declared that nobody could cook like Roxy, anyway.

He helped to dry the dishes and when the kitchen and dining room were in spic-and-span order he drifted into the library again and took some time selecting a book to read, waiting till Roxy should go upstairs for her afternoon nap.

But Roxy sensed that he wanted to be entirely alone for a little, and so she put her head in at the door and said:

"Would you mind if I just run out for a wee while? I promised old lady Sanborne I would run over and write a bit of a letter for her to her daughter. She can't see so good any more, and she finds it hard to write. You won't feel lonesome, will you?"

"No, of course not. I'll be all right. It's very restful here you know, Roxy. I'm just luxuriating in the quiet. Stay as long as you like. There are plenty of books around for me to enjoy."

So Roxy took off her apron and put on her little shoulder cape and hurried away down the road, promising to be back soon. And Barney laid down his book where he could easily assume it again if need be, and went to the window, watching her away down the road until she turned off toward the Sanborne cottage. Then with a sigh of relief he went quickly over to his mother's desk and sat down, as if he were keeping a rendezvous with her.

Tenderly he looked over the whole front of the familiar desk. It seemed so much as usual. Dear mother!

Yet he sensed that it was in more than its accustomed tidy order. His mother had prepared it for him to go over.

And so he began at the right-hand cubby hole, and went slowly, steadily through them all. Neat packets of letters from friends and distant relatives, some since now dead, but letters that were notably friendly and newsy. Barney found himself fancying that his mother had retained these thinking he might enjoy reading them. A few from a favorite and ancient great aunt who had a keen sense of humor and could make the simplest remarks in droll and original language, with grotesque pen sketches illustrating her news. He read them through, and had a feeling that his mother was there, enjoying them with him. What a beautiful thing it was for her to have done, to arrange this little getting-together with her for his homecoming! More than once this thought brought tender tears to his eyes, as slowly he read on from one neat packet to the next, folding them back when he had read them, into their confining bands as he had found them.

Then he came to more recent letters, showing sympathy for her in her illness, cheering her up, speaking of her boy who was fighting overseas. He hurried through those. It wasn't pleasant to him to realize how hard his mother's lonely part had been in this terrible war, sickness and pain, and anxiety for her beloved son!

Then there was a compartment of business letters, clear statements of transactions made since he had left, receipts in full of all bills, so that he might understand what she had done.

He found that she had put all her business into a joint account of herself and her son, so that he would have no trouble, and there would be no delay in his taking over when he came back. It seemed that she had thought of everything. There was even a little book of notes, telling where certain important papers and keys would be found and just what had been put into the safety deposit box in the bank.

He went rapidly through all these business matters, knowing that their time would come in later when he felt strong enough to go into everything with his mother's lawyer, and finally he came to a single letter, bearing his name, his mother's handwriting, a letter from the dead!

With a quick sore break of a sigh almost like a sob he drew it out and began to read.

My precious Barney: This is probably the last letter I will write you on this earth—

His eyes were blurred with tears so that the precious words were almost dimmed by them, and he had to brush them away before he could go on reading. And then he sat back and looked at those words again as if there were glimpses of her beloved face in the written lines. His dear mother, gone from him, but thinking of him at the last minute and leaving him a message—!

Then suddenly there was a sound at the side door, rushing noisy feet, sharp heels clicking across the linoleum of the hall, coming straight and inexorably toward his hiding place. Who could it be? Not Roxy. No! Some intruder!

Instinctively he gripped the precious letter and stared toward the door, which he had taken the precaution to close before he sat down at the desk, but now it was suddenly burst open, tempestuously, as if the intruder would brook no resistance, and a girl with black hair, great dark bold eyes, and a painted face flung herself arrogantly into the room. A girl with sharp red fingernails like claws on her lily white fingers, and a number of noisy clattery rings and bracelets jingling as she moved.

"Well, there you are at last, Barney Vance! I knew I could find you in spite of that old hag of a nurse of yours. I knew she was lying when she wouldn't tell me when you were coming. So I went to the postmaster and found out you were getting letters in the mail, so I just watched my chance when your keeper was out and stole a march on her. And here you are! Darling you look *grand!* And I've come to drag you out of your shell and help you to have some good times and make you forget war. But say, you look wonderful in your uniform! And won't I put it all over the other girls to think I've seen you first! Look up and smile, can't you? I'm Hortense. Your old friend. Your almost fiancée. We were almost engaged before you left, weren't we, Barney? And if it hadn't been for a snooping prowler of a nurse, and a prissy mother, we probably would have been married before you left, too, wouldn't we, dolling?"

And Barney Vance sat there by his mother's desk, with her precious last letter, still unread, gripped fiercely in his fingers, and his knees shaking like any girl's—was it with weakness or anger?—and glared sternly at the unwelcome visitor.

THERE was a long moment of silence while the two took stock of one another, and the young man's glare did not change. The girl was almost taken aback at his silence.

"What's the matter with you, Barney Vance, don't you know me? I haven't changed so much have I? You needn't put on that far-away superior army air. You and I *were* practically engaged you know before you went away to war."

"We were *what?*" asked the young soldier fiercely, hastily wrapping his long fingers protectively about the letter he held, slowly, carefully laying it in its original folds, placing it definitely in an inner pocket, as if he would shield it from contact with the very air this arrogant person breathed.

"Why engaged. Or practically so, don't you know? We would have been openly engaged if you hadn't been so much afraid of your fussy old mother. In fact I think we would have been married before you left if she hadn't interfered with her puritanical ideas, so I went away. It seems funny, doesn't it, that we let people with such funny old-fashioned ideas manage us that way? Sometimes it is easy to see why we needed a war, to wake us up and make us understand that we didn't have to be tied down by such fantastic obedience to our elders. My word! I sometimes wonder how we existed in those days. You certainly must have enjoyed the freedom when you got away from home and in the army among real men, didn't you? But you certainly remember we were practically engaged once."

Barney lifted a haughty chin. The weakness in his knees was beginning to go away now, and anger was surging over him. What right had this girl to barge in here without being asked, as if she belonged, and insult his mother, and the way he had been brought up? He roused to answer coldly:

"Not that I remember," he said brusquely.

"Now Barney, don't be so obtuse."

"It certainly never entered my head that we were anything more than schoolmates. You and I were practically only kids when we last saw each other, too young to give even a thought to engagement or marriage. You must have got your memories mixed." He ended with a distant grin that practically put the whole idea out of the running.

"Now Barney, you horrid thing! What are you trying to do? Take all the romance out of our friendship? And here I've been missing you all this long time, and trying my best to forget you, and I just couldn't do it. I keep thinking back to the time when we were playing games in your dining room and hall and you caught me under the stairs and almost kissed me once, only your snooping old mother came along and stopped you just in time."

The young man arose suddenly, haughtily.

"You will leave my mother out of the conversation,

Hortense. She is too precious to me to allow you to insult her."

"But I wasn't insulting her," laughed the young woman. "I talk the same way about my mother. They couldn't help it that they were born in the Victorian age. But I'm glad I'm out from under, and free to do as I please. And your mother is gone now, and you are free to act yourself. I don't see why you want to be so stuffy about it."

To do Hortense justice she had been to a luncheon and then a tea that afternoon and had partaken of altogether too many cocktails to be quite her normal self, and by this time Barney had begun to recognize that fact, and take the situation in hand.

"Suppose we go out to the porch," he suggested stiffly. "It seems close in here," and he led the way to the side door.

"By the way, how did you say you knew I was in town?" he asked in a formal tone as they went out. "I came at night, and I didn't know anybody knew I was here yet. You see I'm supposed to be under orders to keep very quiet for a while and not see people."

"Oh, *really*? Now Barney that sounds ridiculous! You look just as well as ever, and everybody knows that what a returned soldier needs is a lot of company and a lot of cheering up. That's what I came for, to cheer you up."

"You don't say so!" said the young man with a sardonic grin, though there was still an angry note in his voice. "Well, if you did, please lay off that bunk about our being engaged, for it wasn't true and you know it. Now, come out and see my apple trees in blossom. They're a lovely sight. And don't let's talk about me any more. Tell me about yourself. What have you been doing?"

Barney drew a long breath as the out-of-door air,

sweet with the breath of blossoms, reached him. This was a healthier atmosphere. Somehow it didn't seem as if she *could* quite be so unpleasant out here.

He drew out one of the big rockers tidily tied into white linen covers in Roxy's best style.

"Sit down," he said politely. "Now tell me about yourself. What has happened to you? You know I haven't been home long enough to get any of the gossip. What are you doing with yourself? You're not in uniform, so I judge you didn't join any of the army organizations. I suppose you must be doing defense work of some sort."

Barney was struggling for his best polite manner, in order to awe this terrible girl. If she got interested in talking about herself she might forget to insult his mother, or to claim an undue intimacy for their past. She must be a little drunk or she would never go to such lengths. She was grown up now, and surely she would not insult his mother who had often given her hospitality in the days that were gone.

He drew up another chair, not too near, and settled back wearily dropping his eyelids down for just an instant and taking a deep breath.

"You'll have to excuse me if I don't talk much," he said. "I've been in the hospital for a number of weeks, and I'm just home after a long hard journey you know. You do the talking. What are you? A defense worker, or a nurse?"

"Yes, well, suppose you and I have a little smoke to begin with," said the girl. "This isn't going to be easy for me either, you know. Give me a cigarette. I've used mine all up this afternoon."

"Sorry," said Barney haughtily. "I don't have any. Had you forgotten I'm not a smoker?"

"Now Barney Vance. You don't mean to tell me that

you've been away to war and haven't learned to smoke yet?"

"Oh, does one have to *learn* to smoke?" said the young man amusedly.

"But I thought the army made real men out of boys," said Hortense contemptuously. "I thought surely when you got away from your mother's apron strings you'd turn out to be a real man."

"Oh," said Barney with quizzical lifted brows, "does smoking make a real man out of a boy?"

"Don't be silly," said Hortense. "You know all men in the service smoke and drink."

"Oh no," said the young soldier, "I know quite a number who don't. But don't let's argue about that. You were going to tell me about yourself."

Hortense flung him a sullen furious look.

"Well, get me a drink then, and I'll go on. I've got to have something to hearten me."

"A drink? Why certainly," said the young man rising, "come back with me to the old pump. Roxy always keeps some nice clean glasses on the shelf by the door, and the water is ice cold, you remember."

He rose and led her back to the old pump where they used to drink as children.

"Water?" said Hortense contemptuously, "I want something stronger than that. Get me some brandy or wine or something real. It isn't easy for me to tell my story."

"Sorry," said Barney genially. "You'd better try the water. You'll find it good and cold and quite heartening. I'm quite sure there isn't any other kind of liquor in the house, unless you'd like a glass of milk, or I could make you a cup of tea."

"Heavens! No," said the girl in contempt.

She took a small sip of the clear cold water and flung

the rest on the ground. He took the glass from her, and led the way back to the chairs where they had been sitting.

"But Heavens! Barney! You aren't going to stand for that sort of thing are you, now your mother is gone? Of course I knew she was always a terrific temperance woman, but surely now you can have a mind of your own. You don't have to live on her ideas after you are a man do you? Don't you realize that there is nobody left in this world that you have to *obey* any more? Nobody who can force their ideas and doctrines upon you, nobody to say you have to do anything? I know your mother dominated you, but now you can do as you please."

"And did you think I had no convictions of my own?"

"Of your *own?* Why of course not. You never were allowed to do the things the rest of us did."

"I beg your pardon. That is not true," said the young man gravely. "I was taught to think things out for myself, and decide what was wise and right, after I had looked into the subject carefully. And I have not found that the army life has changed many of those convictions thus formed. But we are getting away from our subject. I believe when we came out here you were going to tell me of yourself. We did not come out here to talk about me and my principles, or convictions of right and wrong. Here's a cushion in this other chair. Perhaps that will make you a little more confortable. Now, sit down and begin. You do the talking. What are you? A defense worker? A nurse?"

Hortense laughed derisively.

"Me? A defense worker! Not on your life!" she drawled. "You couldn't drag me into a thing like that. I couldn't be bothered. I'm just myself, out to have a good time!"

Barney's annoyed eyes studied her derisively for a moment, and suddenly he knew what it was in this girl that his mother had disliked. Mother had been keen. She had seen deep into the character of Hortense Revenal even when she was but a child, and had done her best to guard her son from contact with her.

And yet she was beautiful, after a bold coarse fashion. She had the faculty for taking her own native prettiness and developing it to its fullest extent, even when it meant bringing out her worst traits. She well knew how to lift her lashes and bring an appeal to her great black eyes. She was an adept in all the arts of a woman who wants to appeal to men. And Barney saw now that Hortense was bringing to bear all her arts upon him.

She dropped gracefully into the chair that Barney had brought for her and gave him a ravishing smile.

"Yes?" said the young man. "Well, did you find the good time?"

He watched her as one would watch and study a forward child, although there was nothing at all about Hortense that was childlike. But she quickly snatched the role offered her and began to act it out.

"No," she said dolefully. "I didn't! I did the best I could, but the fates were against me."

"Oh, how is that?" asked the soldier with a quizzical lifting of his brows.

"Well, you see Barney, I got married," she confessed with down-drooping lashes, and an upward quick glance to see what effect that fact would have upon him.

But Barney, not by so much as the flicker of an eyelash let it be known that this was no news to him. He took it quite calmly as if he had not heard it before, and as if it made no difference in the world to him.

"Yes?" he said in a matter-of-fact tone, "well surely that gave you happiness, a good time, didn't it? That is something that is generally supposed to make people very happy."

The black lashes continued to droop, the cheeks were deeply flushed—or was that just the paint? Had they been as red as that before they came out to the porch? Barney wasn't sure.

Then the pouting lips spoke, reluctantly, drawlingly:

"That is what I thought, too," said Hortense dramatically. "But I found it makes all the difference in the world *who* you marry."

"Well, yes, of course," said the young soldier amusedly, "but I would have supposed that you would have looked out for that little matter before you married."

"Well, I thought I did," the girl drawled. She wasn't so good in the role of humility, shameful shyness, but she was attempting it artfully. "He was a rather swell person. At least I thought he was. And reported to be very wealthy in his own right. I couldn't see anything the matter with him, except that he wasn't the man I was in love with. But he had gone off to war and there wasn't anything I could do about that, so I thought I would take the next best thing that offered. You see, Barney, it was really *you* I cared for, but when you went off that way without making me marry you, I was terribly hurt, and I felt I must do something else. Life was simply unbearable without you, and I thought if I could go places and do things and have a good time I would forget you."

"Well, now that's too bad, Hortense. I didn't know that I had had such an unfortunate effect upon you. It never entered my mind that you and I were more than mere acquaintances, sort of playmates, schoolmates, neighbors. But I think you were very wise if you found someone else who was worthy, who might take your mind off of one who wasn't interested in you, you were very wise to marry. Where is he now? Overseas? Is that why your marriage didn't bring you happiness?"

"I'm sure I don't know where he is now," said Hortense sullenly. "That was the first difference we had. I found he was determined to go in the service, and I did simply everything to stop him, but he wouldn't give it up."

"But of course," said the soldier, "anybody that was worth anything would feel that way."

"Oh, of course you would *have* to say that. You're a soldier yourself. But look at you. You came home as quick as they would let you, didn't you?"

"No," said Barney steadily, "I was sent home because I wasn't able to do the job for awhile, and much against my will I was ordered home to recuperate. I'm only anxious to get back and help finish my job as soon as they will let me. But we're not talking about me now. Go on with your story. So he went, did he?"

"Yes, he went. But before he went I found out that he wasn't the wealthy person I had been told he was at all, and he couldn't settle hardly anything on me, and I was about as badly off as I was before. So before he went I got a divorce, but that didn't help me either. It didn't bring me any money at all. And now I'm up a tree, and I thought I'd come to you and see if you wouldn't help me. You were always kind, Barney, and I knew I had to have some real man, someone I could really trust. Will you help me, Barney?" She gave him a languishing, pleading look. "Will you?"

Barney drew a deep breath. What kind of a situation was this going to be for him to get into? What was this girl aiming for anyway? Did she want to borrow money?

Then suddenly he heard a step in the hall, coming from the way of the back door, and Roxy marched out on the porch and stood like a Nemesis looking at the drooping girl.

"And what is all this," asked Roxy sternly. "How did *you* come here?"

Hortense looked up, brushed a few false tears from her big black eyes, and gave Roxy a casual glance, as if she were scarcely worth noticing.

"Oh, hello, Roxy," she said unconcernedly. "What are you? A special kind of a watch dog? You lied to me, didn't you, when I asked you when you expected Barney, but I was too smart for you, and you'll find out I can always outsmart you Roxy. Run along now. We were right in the middle of a confidential talk that's very important. I've been asking for some advice. Hurry along and leave us to ourselves, won't you?"

This interlude was just long enough to give the young soldier a chance to think just what he should do, and when Hortense dismissed Roxy so summarily, and she grimly stood there looking at him questioningly, he turned toward her pleasantly with his old smile.

"Yes, Roxy, I know that I'm off my schedule a bit, but I'm going to lie down right away. I just want to give Hortense an address and then I'll go right upstairs, and perhaps you will give the young lady a bit of your lovely cake and a cup of tea after I'm gone."

Roxy stood there grimly looking as if she would like to say: "I'll do nothing of the kind," but Barney took out his pencil and a card and wrote an address on the card, handing it over to the girl with another smile.

"I'm sorry, Hortense, I'm afraid I'm not up to giving you any advice or help this time, but here is the address of an old friend of mine who is a very wise man, and kindly. Just tell him I sent you to him, and I know he will do all he can for you. Now good afternoon, and we'll probably be meeting again before I go back overseas. So nice to have seen you. I know you'll excuse me under the circumstances!" The tall young soldier made his way quickly upstairs, quietly locking his door when he reached the haven of his own room.

And Hortense stood looking at the card he had given her, and then she looked up at Roxy and made a face at her.

"So! You think you won this time, don't you? But you can't always tell. I got here first, and after this I'll thank you to keep out of my affairs. You certainly can't think you're still Barney Vance's nurse, can you? Surely you know he's grown up, and his mother isn't here any more to back you up."

Roxy held her head high and said in her grimmest tone, "Will you have your tea with lemon or cream?"

"Neither!" said Hortense with a lofty look, "I'm going where I can get something stronger than I can find in this antique dwelling, but you needn't think you can keep that young man under your thumb any longer. He's grown up, and I have my plans for the future."

Then she pranced across the porch, and down the steps to her car, and Barney, watching out the window above, to his great relief saw her drive away.

And Roxy, down on the porch where Hortense had left her, stood and shook a menacing fist at the back of the car as it disappeared in the distance.

6

WHEN the car was out of sight down the road Barney suddenly found himself greatly shaken. It wasn't alone that this girl had barged in on him when he was just about to get a message from the dead, although that of course was the beginning of it. But by this time he was so outraged at what had followed that he had almost forgotten that precious letter which he had managed to thrust inside his coat before she saw it, but it was the whole affair. To think that one of his former associates had turned into such a girl— That she had actually dared to disparage his precious mother's memory, that she had declared herself in love with him, and claimed a former engagement. He was enraged by the whole matter.

He went and sat down in the big easy chair and closed his eyes. He drew a deep breath, and then another, and realized that he was more shaken than he liked to own even to himself. This was no way for a soldier to feel, just because a silly girl, who was really half drunk had said a few foolish things. He should be above caring about things like this. The doctor must have been right after all about his physical condition. If he wanted to get ready to go back to the front he must be able to meet such trifling emergencies, and vanquish them. And it was not a victory just to excuse himself and say he must take a nap because it was in his schedule. He didn't do that when the submarine attacked the ship and for a time they were all in danger of going to the bottom of the sea. Why should he fall before a silly unscrupulous girl? He must get over this. He must go to his stronghold and get strength.

And there in his quiet room, he leaned his head on his uplifted hand and prayed in his heart for a way to meet this situation. For somehow he sensed that this was not just a brief attack by a person outside of his serious world. It was the beginning of a siege, and his experience as a soldier had taught him not to go into combat with *any* enemy, no matter how harmless he seemed, without orders from his commanding officer. So now Barney was asking for orders.

Back in those last few weeks of his strenuous war-life, those weeks during which he had done all that "noble work" in battle that the world over here was beginning to prate about and plan to lift him up as a hero, there had been a comrade, one who though he wore the insignia of high rank, went by the endearing name to his comrades, of "Stormy" Applegate.

Almost at once when Stormy came among their company he and Barney had become friends, had also recognized that both gave allegiance to a higher power than any on earth, had often held brief sweet converse of heavenly ways in the midst of an earthly tumult, to the great heartening of both their spirits. Barney thought of him now as he bent his head to ask for orders, for it was Stormy who had first brought this idea to mind.

"For you know, fella', there are spiritual enemies that come on us unawares, snipers and sharpshooters, hiding behind every tree and shadow, and we're almost apt to think they are one of our own number sometimes, unless we always have our eyes to the Captain. We've just *got* to ask for orders, and then rest it there, knowing we'll be guided right."

Barney half smiled with a tender curve to his lips as he thought of this, and rested his soul about the whole matter. He wished with all his heart that Stormy were there now to talk with him.

For it was Stormy who had been there the night he got his worst wound, that almost finished him and left him lying in the dark among a nest of enemies, dying he thought, and unable to get to his knees and creep away to safety. It was Stormy, who, just back from a noteworthy mission of his own, weary and hungry and all in, Stormy who had gone out to hunt him. Against odds almost impossible he went, and *found* him, quite unconscious, all but dead, and putting him on his shoulder, went toiling back to camp. Stormy had saved his life. Yet when he came back to consciousness Stormy was gone again, out on a secret mission of great danger. For Stormy was a special man, detailed for mysterious missions, seldom expected to return when he went among the enemy. Yet time and time again he had come back, quietly, stepping in among them, greeting them as if he had only been out for a walk, and ready to go again whenever he was sent. When they asked their chaplain how it was he was able to come back, he smiled quietly and said: "Because he goes in the strength of the Lord."

Barney had not seen Stormy now for months. For Stormy had gone away while Barney was still unconscious, on the most dangerous mission of all. Barney had not even been able to thank him for saving his life. And this time he had not come back! It was generally supposed that he had been captured by the enemy, or even killed, or he might be languishing in a concentration camp, or even tortured by the enemy. If they found out in what capacity he had served they would surely wreak vengeance upon him.

"But I don't believe it," Barney had said when they told him about it afterward. And when they asked him why he didn't believe it, he answered with a confident smile: "Because he went in the strength of the Lord."

"Yes, but," said a doubtful listener, "suppose the Lord had something else for Stormy to do this time instead of coming back?" and Barney had answered thoughtfully, "That might be so. But sometime I believe he will come back. I wish it could be before I start for home. I want to thank him for bringing me back to camp. You'll tell him, boys?" And they had promised. Yes, they would tell him.

Barney was wishing for him now. He longed for his understanding companionship, in this new world to which he had come back, where people did not all seem to know there *was* a war, and that life was real. And more than anything he longed to be well enough and allowed to go back to search for Stormy, who had searched for him and brought him back from almost certain death. Now if he might only find his friend, and bring him back!

Of course it had been long days since he had left the place from which Stormy had gone out on his mission. And it had been some time that he had been on the way home, and had had no word. There would be no way perhaps that he could find out if Stormy had come back until he got back overseas again. Or would there? He must look into that. But oh, if he only might go and find Stormy!

These thoughts helped to turn Barney's mind away from his afternoon caller, until his spirit was quieted, and his muscles and emotions had ceased to tremble. Little by little, he went back over the happenings of the afternoon. It was then he remembered his mother's letter, the letter he had not read. His hand went quickly to its hiding place, within the breast of his coat, suddenly anxious lest he might have dropped it in coming up the stairs. No, it was there safely.

He took it out and smoothed the rumpled pages, tenderly, thrilled to hold it now, and to know that he was at last free to read it.

My precious Barney:

This is probably the last letter I will write you on this earth. I know from what the doctor told me, and the way I feel, that I am almost at the end of this life, and ready to walk into the presence of the Lord. *Our* Lord, Barney! You don't know how it thrills me to know that He is truly your Lord as well as mine. It is what I have hoped and prayed for all these years. But although you outwardly acquiesced I was never quite sure that you really knew Him.

So, your last letter, in which you said you had met Him out on the battlefield, and taken Him for your own Savior, has given me joy beyond any I had hoped to know on this earth. Dear boy, it was worth all the dread and agony and suffering of parting from you, of having you so far away, your location a mystery sometimes, danger and death around you constantly. It was worth all that to have this knowledge now, while I am still on this earth, and to be able to thank you for writing it to me at once.

So dear son, I'm rejoicing that you are born

again, and that I am sure we shall meet in Heaven. It just might be, you know, that the Lord Jesus may come for His own while *you* are still on this earth, in which case I'll be coming *with* Him, and we'll meet in the air. But in any case I'll likely be there first. I'll be waiting for you at the gate when you come. And I'm expecting to meet your father there too.

So now dear child, a last bit of warning. Don't let your enemy, the devil, deceive you into getting separated from your Lord. He knows his time is short, and he'll be trying to get you in the subtlest way he has.

And one more thing. Be careful who you marry, Barney! Be sure she knows your Lord. It can make a lot of sorrow for you if she isn't a true believer. And blessings on you both dear lad, when you find the right girl.

Now don't grieve for me, dear. There isn't time. You've a job to do for the Lord. You've witnessing to do in the world. Let your life speak louder than words, and your words be always guided by Him.

And it won't be long, dear lad. It just might be that I may even be allowed to watch you as you come on your way to join me. So good-by till then.

> Your loving mother,
> Mary Graham Vance.

Barney sat a long time with the finished letter in his hands the slow tears streaming down his cheeks. Yes, she had told him not to grieve for her, but he was not aware of the tears. His heart seemed welded to hers, his precious mother! To have this letter seemed a dearer treasure than any gift she could have left him. Her memory had always been dear to him whenever he had been away even for a little while, for he had loved her deeply from babyhood. But now she seemed to be more his than ever in their lives before, for now their love was bound about with the love of Christ who died for them, and in Whom they both believed. It seemed to the young man as he sat there alone in the darkening room, that he grew up in that brief hour, more than in all his years before, even more than he had grown up during the terrible revelations of war, with death and hate stalking the way on every hand. Just to know his mother's God had been as real to her as He had been years ago when she first taught his baby lips to pray, was satisfaction for all his doubts of the past, assurance for the future, even if that future contained more sorrow and disappointment, more war, and sudden death. It would not be long. He had her word for it, that it would not be long. Tenderly he bowed his head and laid his lips on the precious letter, and there in the darkness he prayed:

"Dear God! Keep me faithful. Keep me close. Make my life a true witness. Guard me in *any* temptation, and give me Thy righteousness and Thy strength."

It almost seemed as he lingered with bowed head, that he felt his mother's presence there beside him, her dear hand upon his head, as in the old days. And her Lord's presence filled the room with unspeakable joy and promise.

Then he heard Roxy come slowly, hesitantly up the stairs, and linger outside his door, listening. She would be thinking he was asleep perhaps, and doubtless she had prepared a nice dinner. He must not disappoint her. She would be bringing up a tray pretty soon.

"Coming, Roxy!" he called. "Do you want me?"

"I thought you might be wanting a bite to eat," she said wistfully. "It's all ready. I'll be bringing you a tray."

"No, Roxy! I'm coming down. I've had a good rest, and now I'm coming down to supper. Coming right away!" and his voice had that old hearty ring that cheered her heart.

She eyed him anxiously as he entered the dining room. It couldn't be that his pleasant manner came from any memory of that hussy, Hortense's visit, could it? If that was it she had far rather see him glower.

But he looked her straight in the eye, seeming to read her thought, and beamed out his old grin to reassure her. "She's some terrific brat, isn't she, Roxy? That's what you think, don't you? And I agree with you."

Roxy's face relaxed into smiles.

"Well, I thought if you didn't see I didn't know what I should do. Your mom would be terrible worried."

"Yes, I know, Roxy. Mother never trusted her, and I guess she wasn't far wrong in her reading of that girl, even when she was a kid. But, poor kid! How did she get that way? What was her mother doing? Why didn't she bring her up right?"

"Well, laddie, her mom was a fool, that's why! Your mom knew that when she invited her over here and tried to get acquainted with her, but she never come but once. All she wanted to do when she got here was fool with them bits of playin' cards and eat cakes, and when she found your mom wasn't interested, she went off visitin' where they had big parties and danced a lot. And she had lots of callers, men callers, an' a tough-lookin' lot they was too. That was her life, and that poor child had to suffer for it. Of course it wasn't the child's fault in the first place perhaps, but she certainly has growed up to be a menace to the community. That's what I heard the minister's wife say about her the other day at the Ladies' Aid. She didn't know I heard her, she was talkin' confidential-like to the senior elder's wife, and she said, low-like, 'that girl's a menace to the community. She certainly is. I wish she would get to work doing something worth-while. But I don't know where it would be that she couldn't do all sorts of harm to the people she worked with.' That's exactly what she said. But of course I wouldn't repeat it, only to you. Because I want you to know it's not just because I don't like the girl."

"I understand, Roxy," grinned Barney. "You're only repeating it to me because you want me to understand that *I'm* in danger from her. Is that it, Roxy? Come now. 'Fess-up?"

Roxy giggled, unable to retain her serious poise of gravity, and her anxious expression relaxed.

"Well, yes I 'spose there's lots to say to excuse her from the little bringin' up she had, but still—well, she's a menace all the same. Every last boy she can get her hands on she winds right around her little red-clawed finger. Hardly a one of them has the nerve to turn her down. It's curious. They all see what she is, and yet they fall for her."

"Well, Roxy, I expect she'll bear praying for, won't she?"

Roxy looked embarrassed.

"Well, now,—that sounds like your mom. It certainly does. But all the same I'd say it was safer fer the prayin' ones to be *women*. I just wouldn't trust most of the men I know to get even that close to her, as prayin' would be. I tell you, boy, she's got the devil in league with her, an' no mistake."

Barney looked gravely back.

"I expect she has, Roxy. Most wrong people have, when you come to consider it, haven't they? The only sure way is for the people who are doing the praying to get in league with the Lord, isn't it?"

A surprised light rose in old Roxy's eyes. She almost choked on a bread crumb, and sudden tears came in her kind old eyes. Glad eyes they were now, and no mistake, but embarrassed.

"You—sound—like your little—mom—boy!" she stammered out. "I guess if you talk like that I needn't worry about you any more."

"Oh," said Barney with a twinkle. "Were you worrying about me? Well, that's good of you Roxy, but I'm with the Lord now, Roxy, so suppose you find somebody else to worry about. Say, Roxy, this is swell soup. It tastes like the old times. I shall get well so quick on such fare as you are giving me, that I'll have to be getting my bags packed pretty soon to go back."

"No chance!" said Roxy with a new look of alarm on her kindly features. "You promised me you wouldn't go till the doctor said it was all right for you to go."

There was so much alarm and pleading in her voice that Barney began to laugh.

"Now Roxy, don't you go and get excited. I have no intention of leaving your tender ministry until it is quite all right for me to go, and you'll find the army is pretty rigid about their restrictions. I suspect they'll keep me here far longer than I feel I should stay. However, we haven't come to that question yet awhile. What we've got to concern ourselves about is what we are going to do about these old friends. Are any more of them as far out of the way as Hortense?"

"Well, there's a-plenty of them need prayin' for, if that's what you mean. I reckon prayin' is about as good a way to deal with them as there is, and not quite so dangerous as some other ways. Yes, there's a few girls are followin' in Hortense's ways just as fast as they can. They've got a start kickin' at the traces, an' they think it's smart. You'll see when you get around."

"That's too bad, Roxy. How about Sunny? Is there any danger of her getting the disease? I'd hate to see her growing up to drink and smoke, and talk the way Hortense did today."

Roxy's face beamed into a smile.

"No, Sunny's not like that. She hasn't the time, and wouldn't have the interest if she did have the time. Besides they don't have anything to do with her. They think she's only a stuffy old school teacher. A 'working girl' they call her. They couldn't be bothered with keeping children still and trying to teach them anything."

"That's good!" said the young man. "One less thing to worry about. But say, when is Sunny coming to see us? Does she know I'm here?"

"Well, if she doesn't I suppose somebody'll tell her pretty soon, but I think likely that would be the very reason she wouldn't come. She may have heard you're here, and she's not one to call on a young man, especially when he's a soldier who has been advertised as a hero. Sunny realizes that she was a little child when you knew her, and she's not one to force herself to the front, even to claim an old playmate."

"Oh, so that's it, is it? Well then I see *I'll* have to go call on her. Just find out for me what day and hour would be most agreeable for her to receive me, and I'll lose no time. I want to see how she looks, and make her whistle for me. You don't suppose she'd come over and play ball with me some evening, do you? I think I'll be fit enough for that in a few days. And couldn't we have a tea party out on the terrace? The side away from the road you know, where there couldn't be any intruders barging in on us? I think that would be great!"

Roxy smiled, and entered into the plan eagerly, then hurried away to hand Joel the pail of chicken feed, and to pour the new milk he brought into the shining old pans standing ready for it. Barney finished his meal thoughtfully with some of Roxy's wonderful chocolate cake and peach preserves, and finally went up to his room feeling quite ready for rest. Also he had some praying to do tonight. That was like getting ready for a battle. His heart must be prepared for whatever the Lord was planning ahead. He felt as if his Christian life had taken a new lease, after he had lain dormant so long in the hospital. His mother's letter had given him the impetus, and now he felt he had a job here at home to do, before the Lord would send him back to war again. There was a foe here he could see now, as well as across the water.

And over in the town a couple of miles away, in an ornate boardinghouse, Hortense was laying plans and smiling in anticipation of the way she meant to snare Barney.

7

ABOUT that same time in a bleak detention camp in a far land almost the other side of the world, Stormy Applegate was stealing cautiously in the dead of night out from the surveillance of the enemy. He had done his deadly work that he had come over there to do, had obtained information, and left misleading papers in code behind him in such a way that they would bewilder the enemy, and now he had but to make his getaway. But it was by far the most hopeless looking situation from which he had ever attempted to escape. Only a dummy hastily devised from a log and some of his own garments which he could ill afford to spare on that bitter cold night had made it possible, and even now that might at any minute be found out.

The location was bleak and with little if any spot that might be a shelter. Twice he had almost been discovered, but lying like a log the sleepy guard had not noticed him and had passed on. And now there was barely a brief interval before he would come again. Could he cross that wide stretch of open ground before he arrived? And having crossed it safely would there be another guard more vigilant beyond? Even the stars seemed to have withdrawn their light, and he could not be sure of his direction, although he thought it was ingrained into his very being. Every inch he rolled, every foot he crawled was but an experiment in a great venture for his life.

Wide away toward the homeland somewhere was Barney Vance. Barney had known he was to try this venture sometime in the near future. If Barney were still alive he would be thinking of him now and then, and would lift a real prayer for him. He was almost sure of that.

"Oh God," he prayed under his held breath, "You are here! You'll show me where to go, what to do!"

There! There were the steps of the guard again! Or was that God stepping gently to let him know that He was there?

He rolled another inch or two, tuning his turning with a wind that was blowing. Now! Was he out of range of the guard's path?

But rolled as he was to resemble a log, he lay in a sort of gully where even a quickly flashed light would scarcely recognize him as alive. On and on he persisted, stretched horizontal, stiff with the cold, too stiff to even shudder when he heard the distant clang of steel upon stone, as a guard passed the great rock that loomed behind.

On, on he crept, almost too numb to move cautiously, but not too numb to pray.

"God, if it's Your will, let me get back!"

A single star winked out behind a ragged cloud, and gave him his bearings again. There was another wide expanse of open ground before him to cross. Could he reach a shelter before the dawning?

"Oh God! Do what You want to do with me! It's just Your Stormy, asking to be guided!"

And now ahead was the guard fence. Barbed wire. Plenty of it. Could he manage to separate the strands enough to get through? Were his hands too numb to work them apart?

"God, are You there?"

And now!

There was no sound of guard's steps yet. Perhaps the guard was asleep. Listening cautiously, Stormy worked, wrapping the wires together with his blouse. Could he get through before a guard arrived?

At last the final wire was cut, the opening large enough to creep through, and with his heart thumping wildly again as when he first set out, he came nearer, put a cautious arm through the opening, his head and shoulders, then worked his whole body slowly through!

He looked around. No shadow even in sight yet, it was still very dark. There seemed a hill just below him. Dared he try rolling? Would it make too much noise? He listened again. Was that a step? He must not risk getting caught now.

Carefully he crept ahead, over the little hillock, so slowly that there was scarcely the sound a rubber step would make in the sand. On, on he went, and now and then a star winked briefly to blaze his way.

Off in the distance he could hear a sound. One man calling to another. Had they discovered his absence already? But surely not, for this was the time when the camp was always quiet, the sleepy guards longing to be relieved. He had gone too far and stayed too long not to know the ways of the enemy world into which he had come for the sake of righteousness. A little farther on there were trees and some bushes. If he could make their shelter.

"God, are you there? I'm depending on You. I can't see ahead You know."

His silent thoughts took grotesque turnings. It seemed that he was thinking over his situation, almost aloud, though that couldn't be true, for he was going most guardedly.

"Traveling with God!" he said to himself. "That's what I'm doing. I wonder if any soldier ever thought of that before? Stormy Applegate, if you ever get back to the world, you'll have to tell other soldiers how it is. How safe it is traveling with God. You'll have to tell the world how they forgot to calculate on God, and what He will do for them if they take Him for their Saviour. And I shall certainly tell Barney Vance about this if he is still on this earth and I can find him."

It was almost morning when at last he came within sight of a few forlorn straggling houses. And now, was he far enough away from the camp to dare to risk being seen? And if he should approach one of those ramshackle dwellings, was there anyone there who would dare to hide him? There in an enemy-occupied country? No, there wouldn't be, of course.

On and on he hurried now, in the gathering dawn, making toward what looked like the ruins of a shed at some distance from a shackly barn. If he could get within the shelter of even a few boards, perhaps he could reconstruct his outfit so that he would dare to walk on into daylight for he remembered he was wearing portions of an enemy uniform that he had bargained for from among his fellow-prisoners. Could he pass as one of the enemy? He, an escaped prisoner?

Weary and weak for lack of food, and exhausted with the terrible cold, he plodded on in the lessening gloom of dawn.

He knew enough about the location. He had studied deeply into that. He knew where and when there would be great dangers, he knew of some hazards that were incalculable, he knew his stars when there were any stars to guide him, and he knew how to be exceeding cautious. But there were things he did not know, and then he could only trust to his Guide. So some of those who knew him well, and had watched for him these weeks since his departure, had said he might come back because he went "in the strength of the Lord."

Barney, safe at home, thought about it that night before he fell asleep. He thought of every step that friend of his might have to travel, he thought of the ventures of the way, because he had been in that land himself at one time and had escaped. He knew what there might be to pass through, and so he began to pray about Stormy, until before he slept it came to seem that the way he had envisioned Stormy's path of escape, was a sort of a picture of the way his life might have to go. Even over here in his own land of freedom—supposed freedom—where there were no actual prisoners' camps that might entrap him, no sharpshooters, no enemy guards, no spies and informers to bring him into danger. But yet there was an enemy. The great enemy of his Lord, and he had his scouts out to trap unwary soldiers of a heavenly allegiance. His mother's letter from the dead had warned him of that, had made him see that he must be aware of danger everywhere, and so be watching, and so be trusting in a higher power where he could not see the way clearly himself.

Fantastic thinking. That was what Hortense would call such ideas. But yet, was there real danger for him in that girl? No, he could not think it. Yet he knew of old that she had had power to enmesh one's sympathies, one's lower nature. Perhaps this was one of the temptations that his mother meant when she said the Bible taught that there were some temptations from which one must *flee*.

It had sounded to him as a young boy when his mother taught him, that "fleeing" was what the fellows called "yellow." The idea had not commended itself to him as a child, but now he was beginning to see. His youthful trust had been in his own strength, but he had seen enough of life now to know that there were temptations that one had no right to enter into if there was a way to escape them, and that it wasn't yellow for a soldier, unarmed, to stand around in battle. He must get ready to protect himself if he was to go to war. He must have his armor on at all times, and if he didn't have it on he was to flee from the danger. Well, he was beginning to see. And what was the next direction his mother had taught him about what to do when temptation came? Oh, yes, "Resist." He wasn't to give in weakly. He was to resist. That was what all right-minded people should do in battle.

He was thinking all this out as sleep came down upon him and he dreamed on, tracing Stormy's possible way through danger. He woke up longing to see him. Determined, too, to make his own spiritual walk from day to day with as much caution as if he were Stormy trying to wend his way back in the strength of the Lord, from the power of the enemy where he had gone in his service for the war.

But his last waking thought was a resolve that in the morning he would try to get in touch with Washington and find out if they had any information yet about Stormy. Perhaps he had been heard from, and he felt as if he must know.

Then he knew nothing more, through the long hours of the lovely quiet night, till he woke to another spring morning, gay with the singing of birds.

His first waking thought was of thankfulness that there was still a place where birds could sing, where war had not scarred the earth, where little birds, and even people, could be glad. And then he remembered Stormy. Where was Stormy? Was he still alive? Was he somewhere under torture? God grant it might not be that. He were better dead than under some of the tortures that other soldiers had endured. Would Stormy ever come back? Would he be able to get to a place where the birds were singing and people were really glad? Would the world ever come to a place again where sun could shine without the thought of the gloom of sorrow and bitterness? Would the war be over sometime soon? Oh, if he might but go back now, this morning, and help to bring the end of the war! He felt such a good-for-nothing lying here and luxuriating in the singing of birds when his comrades were over there dying, and Stormy was somewhere doing his part, and he ought to be over there finding Stormy and bringing him back. If he only could find him now, this morning, and bring him here to this place of song. Would the world *ever* come back to peace, and the singing of birds again?

Then he thought of what Stormy would say if he could ask him that. "God is not dead," Stormy would say, with that great wide trusting smile of his. Yes, if Stormy wasn't already in Heaven with the Lord, Stormy was surely saying that somewhere, even if only to himself. Stormy was the trustingest man Barney had ever known, the man who walked continually in the strength of the Lord.

Then he sprang up with almost his old vigor and got ready for the day. There were two definite things he meant to do that day, and somehow the thought of them heartened him. He was going to do his best to get information about Stormy, and he was going to manage somehow to see his little girl friend of past years, Sunny Roselle, and get acquainted with her again. He had a feeling that she would not be as disappointing as Hortense had been. And oh, of course, there were other girls, his old schoolmates. He ought to look them all up pretty soon. Maybe he'd have a party or something, just for the sake of the old days. He would talk to Roxy about that.

But meantime a party for Barney was being arranged with speed and determination by Hortense, and its plan was anything but along the lines in which Barney had been thinking. Hortense meant to make it the smartest gathering that had ever ventured to show its head in the town of Farmdale. But of that Barney knew nothing of course, and was not intended to know, as it was to be a surprise, to welcome him back from the war, and the speedy preparations were carried on behind whispers and a wink or two.

"But don't you think you ought to consult Roxy about this, Hortense?" asked Amelia Haskell, one of the more sensible of the group that traveled after Hortense.

"Consult Roxy? For Pete's sake, *why?*"

"Well, because I've heard that Barney has been terribly wounded, and that he's home on a stiff schedule and has to rest a lot. Roxy would know if it is all right to have a party," finished Amelia lamely.

"Rot!" said Hortense angrily. "Consult that old hag? Not I! Ridiculous nonsense! As if she knew what was good for a down-and-out soldier! What he needs is a little cheering up. He needs to see his old friends, and realize that they are all proud of him and care for him a lot. He needs to laugh and grow merry, and that's what I'm planning for him. Let that old harridan know about our party? Not on yer life! She would put the quietus on it at the start. She wants to keep that young hero all for herself. She wants to put him right back under the thumb his mother tried to fasten on him for life. But I'm setting him free, see? He's a man now and an old nurse can't keep him back and make him walk a chalk line any more. And if any of you so-called 'friends' let her get an inkling of what we're planning, I'm off you for life, and I don't mean mebbe!"

Amelia subsided meekly and no more was dared by anybody else, although several of the girls remembered Barney's decided ideas of right and wrong in his school days. But then, maybe the war *had* changed him, the way Hortense had said. They whispered it over together, but not when Hortense was about.

But Hortense, as a result of these suggestions, merely hastened her plans, and set the time for her surprise party a day sooner. It was necessary that this thing get definitely started before it could possibly be suspected by the victim or else she was practically sure it would never be permitted to come off at all.

So Hortense got busy, and gave her orders, and the very next evening three carloads of young people turned noisily into the driveway of the old Vance house, and after barely waiting long enough to park their cars burst wildly into the house with gay laughter and an improvised number of what they called singing, to make the occasion more definitely a celebration.

And when there was no immediate response from the house, when instead there seemed to be a breathless silence, they looked wildly about and then sang their song over again:

"Happy welcome to you,
Happy welcome to you,
Happy welcome, dear Barney,
Happy welcome to you!"

But, in the meantime, Barney was having a little

private party of his own, out on the side terrace, quite away from the road side of the house. Roxy had given Joel his supper early before he went to his fire company business meeting, and had set a little table on the terrace for Barney and Sunny. They had just finished their dessert when the cavalcade arrived. Barney did not at first recognize what all this other disturbance was about. Not till he looked up and saw the dismay on the face of his guest, and the frown on the face of old Roxy. And just about the time his uninvited onslaught of old acquaintances began to sing their song for the third time, still louder, and more pointedly than before, he began to listen and to recognize what was happening inside the house.

Aghast, he started to his feet flinging down his napkin and giving a startled look, first at Sunny's sweet face suddenly grown grave, and then questioningly at Roxy, to whom he had been so accustomed for years to looking in any time of stress.

It was Sunny who gained her poise first, with her sweet smile dominating the situation.

"I think," she said in a very low voice, "that you are about to have a surprise party, and the best thing for me to do is to vanish. Go in there quickly, Barney, before they swarm out here and spoil everything."

Then Barney came to himself.

"Vanish? Not much you won't vanish! Come on in with me and help me through this situation."

He put out his hand to take hers, and lead her in, but she stepped back and eluded him quickly.

"No, I mustn't Barney. I wouldn't fit with them, and I would be much misunderstood. Really! Go quickly! They mustn't know about this, you know," and she swept her hand toward the table. "Good-by, I've had a lovely time!" and suddenly she was gone! Vanished! Just

8

TO say that Barney was annoyed at the sudden turn of events was putting it mildly. He had been looking forward to a pleasant evening getting acquainted all over again with the little girl, Sunny, and trying to reconcile her with the charming grown-up Sunny who seemed so fittingly to be called "Margaret" as Roxy had been calling her that evening. And now she had to disappear and he must go in and be gracious to a lot of nitwits in the other room who had come to do a little hero-worshiping and look him over, at the instigation of that brat of a Hortense. For he at once jumped to the conclusion that Hortense was at the bottom of this.

Well, he would go into the other room and greet them for half an hour perhaps, and then, afterwards, they *might* leave in time for him to run down to Sunny's house and apologize for letting her go home in that unattended way. And he meant also to find out just why she hadn't stayed.

Ah, but he was reckoning without the present-day knowledge of Hortense and her ways.

So he put on his dignity in haste and stalked into the

side door, that opened into the back hall from the terrace. He reflected as he passed their supper table that it was well they had finished the strawberries and ice cream they had been eating for dessert, and there were very few dishes for Roxy to get out of sight, since she had taken the tray in with her.

So he entered the hall as they finished the last line of that awful song again, and assumed a surprised attitude, looking at them curiously, identifying a few of the men, and recognizing some of the others, Hortense, right in the forefront, in a very scant and sophisticated evening frock. For an instant he was so angry at her that she should have pulled off a thing like this without warning, he could scarcely trust his voice to speak. But he quickly controlled himself and went forward, a distant smile upon his face.

"Well," he said formally, "look who we have here! Old friends, come to call! Say, that's kind of you. Come in and sit down, won't you? This really isn't my birthday though, you know, so you needn't overwork that poor old song any longer. Now, let me see, do I know you all? Some of you have changed a lot, haven't you? Grown up, isn't that it? This one is Amelia Haskell, isn't it? Yes, I thought I knew those big gray eyes. And the Wrexall twins! Yes, I'd know you anywhere. And—say, don't tell me you are Hortense Revenal? Why, I'd hardly know you in that glad rag. Isn't that one of those they call a 'smaht fwock'? And here is Lucy Anne, and Jan Harper! Why, I'm doing pretty well identifying my old friends, don't you think? And my word! There's Cap Withrow. How'd you get here? I thought I heard you were in Africa, or somewhere overseas. And Hank! Good night! how many feet do you grow a month? What size of shoes do you wear? You've grown so tall I have to look up to you, now."

So he went on down the line, cheerily, a word for everybody, and for the moment in perfect control of the situation, as they all stood watching him, studying him, recognizing the changes that had come to him, in gravity, in assurance, in experience. Yes, he was different. Even Hortense could recognize that.

Yet Hortense wasn't quite satisfied with the state of things. She wanted to be the center of the show, right from the start, in fact the whole show, in her new and expensive gown that wasn't paid for yet, and had cost her more than she could afford. She wanted to dominate the evening, and here she was only one of the whole bunch, and she could see by Barney's manner that he intended to keep her so. She was not to be allowed to exercise her possessive powers, not if he had anything to say about it. But she was only the more determined to show him. He couldn't put her off like that when she had got this whole thing up to honor him. She would show him!

"Won't you all sit down? I guess there are chairs enough in here, aren't there?" said Barney. "It looks like we ought to have a regular old time talk-fest, doesn't it? Hank, you and Cap bring some of the dining-room chairs in here, won't you? You remember where the old dining room is, don't you? Same room where we used to play blindman's-bluff in the past ages. Amelia, you take the piano stool. We'll be wanting to sing some of the old songs pretty soon, and you'll be handy there to play for us. Martha, take the big chair next."

He was certainly taking things in his own hands, and doing it very thoroughly. Hortense realized that she must get busy and take control.

"Hi, Hank!" she called, making a picturesque trumpet of her pretty white hands with their gleaming red claws, and flashing jewels. "Get busy and bring the gramophone in. We want to get started on our evening.

We came to have a good time, you know. This is no church social. We want to dance."

"Oh, we don't need a gramophone," said Barney coolly with one of his old-time grins. "Don't try to be so sophisticated. We're all just hungering and thirsting to do some of the old-time things we used to do. How about playing 'I have a rooster for sale,' and 'Drop the handkerchief,' and 'Here we go round the barberry bush,' and a few of those. Nothing like the old-time childish games to take off the stiffness. And then, pretty soon we ought to sit down and really get acquainted over again. Call the roll and find out where everybody is and what you all have been doing. Suppose we do that first. I'll call the roll as far as I can, and then somebody else take over and finish, till we've got around. When you answer tell where you are, where you've been, what you've been doing and what's likely ahead of you, and when we get done I'll be caught up on my home history. Hank, we'll begin with you!"

Hank grinned and answered briskly, "Working in a defense plant, got called, had my physical, they found I had a bad heart and turned me down, so now I'm a riveter."

"Next! Cap. What of you?" asked Barney quickly.

"Oh, I wanted to be a flier the worst way, but they found I had something the matter with one eye, so now I'm a machinist. Over at Tennally's, fiddling with screws for airplanes, when I wanted to fly the planes." He grinned comfortably and somewhat ruefully, and one of the girls called out "Lucky boy!" That was Rowena Lake. Barney gave her one quick withering glance and passed on to the next.

"Arta Perry, what of you?"

"I joined the Army Nurses. I'm leaving tomorrow morning for my new location."

Barney gave her a keen once-over, decided the uniform was becoming, and turned to Hortense who stood next to her.

"And you, Hortense?" He asked the question casually, making her just one of many, instead of a special one, and Hortense resented it. She tossed her head indifferently.

"Oh, I'm an entertainer for the boys at the center," she said, quite as if it bored her to even think of it. "But say, for heaven's sake, Barney, how long are you going to keep this up? We came here to show you a good time, and you're just spoiling it all."

"Oh, I'm sorry," said Barney gravely. "I was under the impression I was the host to my guests and ought to do my best to entertain them. I think we ought to get acquainted all over again, though, don't you? It won't take long and then we can go on from there."

"Oh, well, make it snappy then," said Hortense. "We've got a program of our own, you know."

"Oh, I see. Well, we'll hurry this up. Who's the next one?"

Two dimpling grinning girls in nurse's uniforms were next, and they answered the roll call interspersed with giggles.

They went down the line rapidly, crisply, each telling a bit about himself, briefly, sometimes half in the spirit of fun, and some more gravely, and when the last guest had answered the roll call, Barney called out, "That's good. Now we can go on from here and enjoy ourselves more intelligently. How about it, Hortense, will you take over and let me sit down?"

"Oh, but we haven't heard from you, Barney!" called out one of the Wrexall twins. "It's time for you to give an account of yourself now!" and a chorus of the others called out, "Yes, yes! A speech from Barney. Where have you been, and what have you done?"

"Oh," said Barney, "I suppose I *am* still one of the old crowd, but it hadn't occurred to me I would have to give account of myself. Well, here goes. I'll make it brief. The most notable thing that has happened to me since I went away was that one dark night on a lonely shore, a smashed plane on the ground behind me, crouching enemies behind every tree, and nothing before but a big lonely stretch of sea, not even a foxhole to hide in, out there in a place like that I met God, and got to know Him. It was the greatest thrill that ever came to me, and still is. Sometime I'll tell you all about it, if you care to hear, but it's too long a story for tonight. Now, fellows, who's going to take over? Shall we sing some of the old songs?"

"Oh, for heaven's sake!" said Hortense angrily, "Hank, you and Cap go get the eats and drinks. I'm near dead for a drink myself, and I guess you're all pretty well fed up with this gruesome start. Now Barney, you sit down and try to realize we came to welcome you home again, and give you the honor due to a hero of war."

"Oh," grinned Barney, "don't bother about that hero stuff, just be yourselves, my old friends! But excuse me a minute, I'll go out and help. Fellas, hold up a minute, I'm coming!"

Amid the immediate protests of the girls, he flashed out into the kitchen, hoping to find Roxy.

There she was, getting out glasses, trays and napkins.

"Roxy, can you get us some coffee, or lemonade or something?" he called in a quick, low voice as he vanished out the side door and streaked it across the lawn, arriving at the line of parked cars almost as soon as the committee Hortense had sent out.

Two large baskets of cakes and sandwiches were

deposited on the lawn beside the gramophone and Hank was just reaching farther into the car, and edging out the case of liquor they had brought along.

Barney gave it a scrutinizing glance, and put out a protesting hand.

"It won't be necessary to bring that in, fellas. Roxy's getting something for us. Come, take your gramophone and your eats, and let's get back." Barney's hope of getting to see Sunny again that night was fast vanishing.

Hank paused and looked at his host.

"Sorry, Barney, but I guess I have to take this in. Hortie'll have all kinds of a fit if I don't. She was very particular about this."

"Well, I guess we can stand a few fits, if it comes to that. Hortense knows how I feel about that. You see we just don't serve that here, so you needn't bring it in. Come on, fellows!"

So the three went in together, silently. Hank had it in mind to tell Barney what a fuss Hortense had made to get that liquor, and how she had made everyone contribute to it, but then he decided not to say anything, and they walked along for the most part in silence, only Barney now and then making a cheerful remark, and so they arrived in the house.

They put the four baskets of cakes and sandwiches in the kitchen where Roxy took grim possession, Barney seized the trayful of brimming glasses of fruit punch fragrant and luscious, and assigning Hank and Cap to the other two trays, marched into the living room and straight over to Hortense. She looked up hopefully, and he bent and tendered her a glass.

"You were thirsty, lady?" he said mischievously, and Hortense looked up in surprise.

She reached an eager hand to the glass, then caught the fragrance of well-blended fruit, and frowned.

"Why, what's this?" she asked, drawing back her hand. "This isn't what I sent you for, Hank. What are you trying to put over on us?"

"Try it, lady," urged Barney with his old-time grin, "I think you'll find it quite drinkable. Or, if you prefer coffee, I think that some is on the way."

"But I brought . . ." burst forth Hortense in a vexed tone. "Hank, I told you to bring . . ."

"Yes, I know," said Barney. "But don't blame Hank. I told him we don't serve that here, and I thought you would understand."

Barney flashed her a pleasant confident smile, and went on passing the tray to the other girls. They seized eagerly upon the glasses for everyone knew that anything Roxy had concocted would be something extra, and so it was.

Several of the girls had slipped into the kitchen as the boys came in with the trays, and now they began to march in with plates and napkins and platters of sandwiches, and it was presently a happy young crowd that chattered away, and ate up every sandwich and crumb of cake, and drank the seemingly inexhaustible cups of coffee, and glasses of fruit lemonade, until, before long, no one thought any more about that liquor except the girl who had schemed to bring it just for the sake of forcing Barney to drink. She knew how Barney's mother had felt on that subject, and it was her great desire to bring the young man to the place where he would go against those queer old-fashioned principles of the woman who had so annoyingly dominated him all his life, and who now even in her death was holding him from things that Hortense loved. Things she knew if she could just break down there would be some hope of bringing him to her feet.

But the evening wore on, and the gay young crowd

grew cheerful in the memory of the dear old days, and forgot the glum Hortense who had retired disapprovingly into a corner and taken little part in the merriment of the rest.

Only once she came out of her corner and started that gramophone noisily on its way, and then made the boys move back the chairs, and started dancing with one of them. Soon a few others joined her, but for the most part they were interested in a story Barney was telling, and the dancing, being rather forced just then, languished for lack of participants. Somehow Barney was having a queer effect upon that young crowd, who of late had most of them followed Hortense in everything she did. To have one come in who definitely ignored her lead and openly, pleasantly defied her; Hortense herself could not believe that this was really happening. And yet with it all, Barney was his old merry engaging self, not long-faced nor self-righteous, not goody-goody, nor conceited, not mamma's-little-boy, still tied to her apron strings, though she *was* gone to another world. Certainly he was not a sissy, but a strong man who had ideas, and what he called principles of his own; who had made his mark in the war and won trophies, and honorable mentions, and been unafraid in danger, done deeds of daring, and had outranked many who seemed harder and tougher than he when he was a lad. And yet now even Hortense saw this, although she could not explain it. What was it made him so quietly firm in certain matters? And why had he so deliberately foiled her attempts to put on the kind of party that she knew his mother would not have enjoyed having in her home? Had it been just for hatefulness? No, somehow he did not seem that way, for there was in his manner a gentleness and strength that she did not remember to have noticed in his childhood. And yet she was frantic that her plans had been spoiled, like a little pink and golden wraith in the mist of the evening.

Barney gave a despairing motion toward her, started to call, but Roxy shook her head.

"Hush! Go in there quick! She's right! They mustn't know about this!" and she caught up the trayful of dishes that was standing on a chair and vanished into the kitchen.

and everyone could see that she had failed in putting over this worldly kind of a party in a house where the whole atmosphere had always been what she called, even in her childhood, "old fogy."

Hortense watched the young man as the evening went on, and saw his continued pleasantness and courtesy under what she sensed must be trying circumstances for him. She didn't care for that of course, but she couldn't understand what kept him strong and sweet through it all.

They began to sing after a time, Amelia, seeing Hortense defied, dared to start a little something on her own initiative, and sitting at the piano let her fingers run into several old-time songs that caught the whim of the crowd and made them hum together, and finally pour out their voices in a big peppy chorus.

"School days! School days!
Dear old golden rule days!
Reading and writing and 'rithmetic,
Taught to the tune of a hickory stick!"

How it rang out and stirred the heart of Roxy and Joel, disapprovingly cleaning up in the kitchen.

Then came "Put on Your Old Gray Bonnet." They were such very old songs that Roxy marveled those young things should know the words, even though the radio had been reviving them now and again. And there was "Juanita" and "Annie Laurie" and "Old Black Joe" and "Swanee River." Sometimes Amelia's nimble fingers would tinkle out the beginning of another and all would take it up, sometimes a girl's voice would be ready with a new one, ere the last one was finished. It was a gay bright ending to a queer evening, and Barney, as he sang, looked about upon them all and wondered why Sunny hadn't stayed. As he continued to think about it he realized how far superior she was to most of the girls there. Even the few minutes they had been together this evening at supper had told him that. Yet some of those girls had good faces, though some were vapid, some conceited, and some just idle pleasure-loving kittens who merely wanted a good time out of life. The boys were not much. That is, the ones who were here. They were the henchmen of such girls as Hortense, who went their errands and were satisfied to be their humble escorts when more desirables were not at hand. And yet, if those same boys had gone off to war, nine out of ten of them would have learned the serious side of life, and be ready to do some purposeful thinking.

Somebody suddenly started "The Old Rugged Cross," and strange to say, even in that crowd, everybody seemed to know the words and rather liked to sing it, although he could see Hortense's lips curl in scorn. He felt sure that if she were a singer she certainly would have chimed in with some modern jazz just in contrast. Then, as the last notes of the hymn died away Barney struck up in his clear beautiful baritone:

"Abide with me: fast falls the even tide;
The darkness deepens; Lord with me abide!"

It was a song he had sung often when overseas, when he was about to go into a dangerous engagement. It seemed to him now as he sang it that his song, as it had often been before, was a prayer. He had a passing thought that he was perhaps in as much need of help now as he had ever been in battle.

A strange dark look came into Hortense's eyes as she watched his face while he sang, but he was not looking at her and did not notice, and so he sang the verses as he remembered them from childhood, till the last line when the final word died away.

It was very still in the room for an instant, and then the silence was suddenly broken with as distinct a snap as if the quietness had been as brittle as a glass tube, that fairly broke at the new sound. It was Hortense, of course. She made a restless impatient movement, shoving her chair back sharply to the bare floor beyond the rug, and arose with decision and a disagreeable sneer on her lips.

"I'm going home!" she announced sharply. "I'm just fed up with this sob stuff, and I have to run up to New York in the morning for a shopping trip so I want to save my strength. Good night! Are any of you coming with me?" and she sailed out of the room toward the front door with her head high.

"Oh, cut it out, Hortie," shouted one of the young men who had come with her, "we're just getting into the fun. You said you were going to stay late."

"Sorry," said Barney, "have I been monopolizing the program too much? Suppose I sit back and rest awhile and you take over, Hortense. How about your giving us a solo yourself? Seems to me I remember you had a good voice when you were a kid. What numbers have you got? I'd like to hear you sing again, and then meantime you can be thinking up what you want to do next. Come on, be a good sport and sing us some songs, Hortense."

Hortense paused in the doorway, and surveyed the young soldier, good-looking and courteous in his well-fitting uniform. Was it really worth while? Then Barney turned on his winning smile, and she suddenly resolved to try again. She simply *had* to conquer him now, or they would all see that she had failed. And besides, she was flattered to be asked to sing. She was proud of her voice.

So she fixed her languishing gaze on Barney's eyes for a moment, and then drawled:

"Oh, well, I don't mind waiting long enough to sing for you, since you ask it," she said it with the air of conferring a great favor. Hortense was exceedingly fond of herself. She would do almost anything to glorify herself.

Amelia arose from the piano stool as if she felt she ought to be apologizing for having been there, and Hortense sat down with an air, entirely aware of the lovely lines of her expensive evening dress, glad that there was really an opportunity at last to display it to advantage. She had been showing off, either herself or her possessions, ever since she was born.

Hortense's white fingers fell daintily upon the keys, as if she idly searched among the notes to find what she would sing.

At last she looked up.

"Just what do you want me to sing?" she asked Barney loftily, as if her repertoire included anything he could possibly ask, but Barney only smiled:

"I'd like to hear the song you like best to sing," he said graciously, and Hortense settled down to work with a look of satisfaction on her sharp, hard young face.

Hortense had a thin shallow voice, with a distinct whine to it, and moreover was inclined to the mournful desolate self-pitying tone that so many of the current crooners affect. Barney, as he watched her wondered why she did not know that her voice was unpleasant. Then he put on an attentive attitude and let his thoughts wander off to other things.

The other girls in the room sat about politely, and he studied each face. Amelia's was quiet and humble, not much sparkle there, some of the others were very pretty, but yet didn't seem to have much behind the prettiness.

Or was it because he had another face in his thoughts with which he was comparing them? Well, that was silly. He hadn't been seeing Sunny but a very few minutes, and that while they were eating their supper out on the terrace, and at such close range that he could not stare at her and really know how she did look. Just a lovely, rose and golden look, with a glance in her eyes that one could not help trusting. Well, this was silly, only he wished this party would get itself over and let him go to sleep and wake up to a new day when he might perhaps get a chance to go and see Sunny and study her a little more.

9

FROM that time on the party became quite gay, to Barney's utter weariness.

But in spite of that fact he was up early next morning and down to breakfast much to the surprise of Roxy who had expected him to sleep late, and was meditating an especially tempting breakfast, later, when he woke up.

But he told her all he wanted was just what she and Joel had, some of that nice looking oatmeal, with real cream, and a cup of her coffee.

"Would I embarrass Sunny if I went down there this early?" he asked suddenly, while he was enjoying the scrambled eggs she heaped upon his plate, and the crisp buttered toast she produced after the oatmeal and orange juice she insisted upon. "I can't seem to settle to anything," he went on, "not even resting, till I apologize for the way I let her run off alone in the dark."

"Oh, she didn't mind that," laughed Roxy, "she's used to running around alone. And it didn't seem to me you had much choice about the matter. It was Sunny ran away from you."

"Yes, but I should have stopped her somehow. Why did she do it, Roxy?"

"She was right, Barney boy. You don't realize. If she had stayed here that crowd would have made her feel very uncomfortable. They would either have taken it for granted she was here as a sort of servant, helping me out, or else they would have judged her by themselves and made it appear that she was running after you. I thought it quite sensible of her to go."

"But why should they treat her that way, Roxy? They're no better than she is. They're none of them anything great. I'm sure teaching school is just as honorable and necessary in these times, as riveting, or going around entertaining soldiers home on leave, or any of the other things those girls are doing."

"Wouldn't you think so?" assented Roxy. "But would you believe it, those other girls almost ignore her. You wouldn't think she was brought up in the same town. And it's just because she hasn't forged ahead and forced herself into all their silly parties. She doesn't drink nor smoke nor dance the night away. She has too much real work to do. Of course there's a few others wouldn't care so much to be frivolous, if they didn't feel they had to copy that poor simp of a Hortense. And why, I can't understand. She hasn't got any money, and she isn't good-looking. I believe it's just because she's dared to do things and take the lead and laugh at them if they don't follow her. She dared to get married in a hurry, and then she dared to get divorced, and she's sort of made herself the fashion although she calls it 'smaht.' And there's Sunny with her sweet delicate lips clean and smiling, without any paint on them but her own healthy skin the way God made them, and they won't speak to her, unless they want her to do something for them that they can't do themselves. And they go around with their great wide thick lips all staring bright red and horrid, and disgusting. I've often wondered why they paint them up so thick and wide. They look as if they were swollen and bleeding."

"Yes, they do, don't they?" laughed Barney. "It isn't a bit attractive. A good many fellows I know laugh at the way the girls are painted, just to attract attention. But you didn't answer my question. Do you think it's too early for me to run over to Sunny's house? Would I be interrupting some work she ought to do? This is Saturday. She wouldn't be teaching school today would she?"

"No, there's no school today, and I don't think she'd mind your being there even if she was busy. She'd probably let you help her if it was anything important she couldn't leave till another time. Run along and see Sunny, and if you want to bring her back here to a meal any time just feel free to do it. Sunny's a dear child, and I'm fond of her."

So Barney finished his breakfast and started out eagerly, reflecting with satisfaction that he was glad his guests of the night before wouldn't have waked up yet, at least not many of them, and would therefore not be on hand to see where he was going.

As he walked along the sunlit road he heard the birds singing high in the sky, some far in the distance, and in spite of himself his heart was filled with a grave delight. The quiet air, filled with sunshine, the birds everywhere. Oh, it was good to be at home again where there were no sounds of bombing, no tenseness in the air, no fear of what was going to develop during a day, or what would happen on the morrow! No feeling of desperation, when comrades and friends moved out of sight for an engagement from which some would, in all probability, never return. Oh, it was good to be in a land of peace for a little while! Though somehow last night's gaiety did not appeal to him as good. It had seemed that all his former friends were just children yet, where he had left them when he went away, seeking fun and more fun, thrills, and greater thrills. They had not yet reached the place where they cared much about anything that did not affect them personally, that would bring them a better time, a forgetfulness of life. It didn't occur to them that there might be disappointment in the world, and that there were grave serious things to think about. It was a sense of the nearness of death that brought that; and while they were eager about doing things in an important way, especially if they could wear a uniform, they did not in the least recognize what war was like. To them war was just a big game, to win at all odds, and to tell tales about afterwards of their own prowess.

He looked across to the soft green hills. Off there, just beyond the woods, gleamed the white stones of the little cemetery where his mother's body had been laid, and a tender look came into his eyes. He hadn't been up there yet. Some day he must go, pretty soon. But he had been better taught than to do honor to a mere human body from which the spirit was gone. He did not think of that spot up there on the hill as being sacred for his mother's sake. It was only her tired-out body that lay there. Her spirit was with her Lord. She had taught him that. Yet he looked toward the white stones that gleamed in the morning sunshine, and realized that he would want to mark the place where they had laid her with a stone bearing record of her birth and Home-Going, and some verse from God's word that could be a testimony for a chance reader who might be unsaved. Yes, even though he knew it was but her tired body that lay there waiting, like old garments that were no longer needed, it brought tender thoughts.

And then he came in sight of the Roselle farm. A

pleasant, wide, rambling white house, gleaming in the sun, nestling in its tall setting of old elms. It had such a homey, properous look, as if it had just newly been finished, although he knew it had been there many years. How well they had kept it up, even in these hard wartimes. And Sunny's father must have been the only one to do the work, since Sunny's brother went into the service.

He was almost to the hedge-bordered lane that led to the house when he saw a lithe young figure flash out of the kitchen door carrying a clothesbasket. She put it down on the stone pavement by the pump and stooping, took out a roll of cloth and shook it out till it filmed into a curtain, thin and white. With firm brisk fingers she fastened it to the clothesline just a step away. Then she stooped and took out another roll and treated it the same way, till the row of curtains were blowing gaily in the morning breeze.

Barney was walking slowly, watching her. Apparently she had not noticed him yet, and most of the time her back was toward the road. It seemed that she was too busy to be watching what went on in the world about her.

He had not reached the turning of the lane before she had the basket empty and all those curtains blowing on the line. Then she swung around and hurried up the steps to the kitchen door, and in out of sight without even looking down toward the road. Had she seen him or not? He didn't think she had. And yet, she wasn't a girl who was always trying to attract attention to herself. Besides she wouldn't likely be expecting him to call so very early.

With quickened step he turned up the lane and hurried to the house, tapping at the door where he had seen her vanish, and calling, "Sunny! Sunny! Where are you?" Then he heard her mother's voice calling from an inner room.

"Margaret, someone is calling you at the kitchen door. Won't you answer the knock? I'm not fit to be seen. I've just spilled some milk down the front of my dress."

And then he heard Sunny's quick step hurrying to the door.

"Oh!" she said, a glad light coming into her face. "Barney! It's you! And out so early! I thought you were supposed to be an invalid who had to sleep late."

Barney grinned.

"Not when I have something more important to do," he said. "Did I come too early? Will I be in the way? If I am just tell me the truth and I'll go outside and sit in the sun till you have time for me, but I simply couldn't stand it until I came to apologize for letting you go home that way last night."

The twinkle came into the girl's eyes, just as when she was a tiny child.

"Oh, but you couldn't help it," she laughed, and her laughter was like a string of silver bells. "I know how to vanish. And then it was getting dark. Besides, it wouldn't have been good."

"Yes? Well, as soon as you get done what you're doing you've got to sit down for at least five minutes and tell me just why it wouldn't have been good. I thought it would, and I still think so, but out of deference to you I have tried to be reconciled till I could get here and have it explained."

The girl laughed brightly again.

"Well, you see, I'm not in their crowd. Those girls have no use for me, and I'm afraid maybe I haven't felt very friendly toward them. They are not at all in my class. We just don't fit, that's all. But—they are *your* friends. I don't want to say anything against them. We just don't fit."

Barney was studying her sweet face as she talked. He saw she was trying to be nice about it and not to say too much. Trying to be polite, and not to seem self-righteous. He watched her gravely till she stopped and gave him a grave questioning look.

Barney grinned.

"Having spent an entire evening with that crowd I can well understand that you don't fit," he said fervently. "And I'm *glad* you don't! I would be disappointed in you if you did. Oh, there are two or three of those girls who aren't so bad, might be all right if they were in the right company, but just now they aren't. Yet all the same I'm sorry I had to let you go off that way unattended. It was not in my plan to have my own party end up that way."

Sunny's eyes lighted.

"Oh, that was all right," she said demurely, "but— thank you. It is nice you cared."

"Cared?" he said. "Why of course I cared, and I still care. Aren't you my little pal, Sunny? Did you suppose I could forget that? Only they call you Margaret, now, don't they? I heard you called after I knocked. Was that your mother's voice? *Margaret!* It fits you. I like it. I've always liked that name, only I'm afraid I shall always think of you as Sunny! Little Sunny!"

He gave her a clear admiring steady look, that seemed to be searching her through and through, and held her own glance for the moment, while the rosy color swept up into her lovely face, and then her eyes went down.

How lovely she was, he thought as he watched her for another long minute in a sweet silence, and then he spoke:

"And now, what were you going to do, and may I help? Were you going to hang those curtains? They have to be ironed first, don't they? I can iron. My mother taught me, and then we often had to do some of that in training. And how about the windows? Don't they have to be washed? I could do that! I used to be good at it."

"Oh, but those things can all wait," said Sunny with a golden look. "You have come to call on me, and I'm going to have a nice time. I'll do the work when this is over. I'm just going to enjoy your company now."

"Oh yes?" he asked comically, "not if the court knows herself. We'll do the work first and then we'll have earned a good time. We might even take a long walk to the woods and have a picnic. But the work must be done first. Where do I find the rags and brushes to clean the windows?"

"But no!" said Sunny with a troubled look. "You with a lovely uniform and all those wonderful decorations, washing windows! You'd get all messed up."

"No," said Barney decidedly, "I'll not get messed up. The army taught me to do work and not get messed up. And besides, young lady, you had your way last night, cutting my party short and running away in the dark, and now it's my turn! I say we're going to work first, and then play, and I mean it! May I take off my coat?"

"But—" said Sunny, with still that troubled look.

"What are you two arguing about?" said Mrs. Roselle, suddenly appearing at the door of the dining room. "Isn't this our old friend Barney, Margaret? Why do you sound so dictatorial?"

"But mother, he is insisting on helping me. He wants to wash windows! Imagine it. With that handsome uniform on."

"Mrs. Roselle, I am only offering to help Sunny,— Margaret. We'll get the work out of the way, and then we'll go and play, have a picnic maybe. Isn't that fair?"

"Splendid!" said the mother with a smile. "I'll get him

an apron, and he can roll up his sleeves. You'll have fun working. There isn't so much to be done. I've started the ironing machine, and you'll have the curtains up in a jiffy. Barney will be a lot happier that way, I know, for I know how his mother brought him up," and she trotted away and brought him a big apron that enveloped him. He tied it on and went around admiring himself in the crisp blue gingham folds, so that the whole argument ended in a good laugh, and then they went to work with a will.

"But I thought you were an invalid, sent home to get well, and here you are working as hard as if you were fighting a battle," said Sunny, still troubled.

"I'm afraid, madam, your education has been neglected. I'm afraid you haven't a very good idea of what a battle would be like as compared with a little job of washing a few windows with the garden hose and all these brushes to help."

So, with laughter and song they went to work. For the ironing machine was close at hand where the windows had to be washed and they had a lot of time to talk. And then they got to the subject of whistling, and Barney asked her all about that, and demanded to hear her whistle, and Sunny began to whistle.

Barney was amazed. He had always felt no girl could really whistle, but Sunny could whistle as well as he had ever been able to do it.

"I'm proud of you," he said. "I never found a boy that could do it that well, and I've tried to teach several of them. But you do it like a bird."

She looked at him with a quick flush, surprise and pleasure in her gaze.

"I never expected you to say that," she said quietly. "I practiced and practiced, and I never could get Roxy to say I did it as well as you did but once. You can't think what that used to mean to me when I was a child. I thought your whistle was the sweetest music I had ever heard anywhere. It seemed to me better than the bird's singing."

"You certainly were a cute little trick," said Barney with quick appreciation. "And how have they kept you so unspoiled? All the other girls are so illuminated that you can scarcely recognize your old acquaintances."

Sunny smiled.

"I guess I'm just old-fashioned," she said. "I don't admire faces that are not natural. I like God's plan best."

"So do I," said Barney with vehemence. "I can't see why anyone can like it. Well, I certainly like you as you are. You seem so much as you were, and not as if you were trying to be 'smaht' as Roxy says." And then they laughed, and presently Mrs. Roselle came back into the room.

"Come, children, you've worked enough for one lovely spring day. Enough for a soldier home on sick leave, and a busy little schoolma'am. Besides I've got your lunch all put up and if you're going on a picnic it's high time you got started. It's April you know, and you're liable to run into a shower or two by afternoon. Come now, put your work away and hurry off."

"Oh, but we're almost done, dear," said Barney in his old familiar way. "I've just one more window curtain to hang, and then the room is done."

"Why, so it is! And how beautiful it seems! My, that's wonderful to get these windows all cleaned so early in the season. Soldiers are great workers, aren't they, Margaret?"

It seemed a happy thing to Barney to be there with those two, his mother's old friend and her little girl, in the simple home life doing honest work, and being happy together. It comforted a lonely spot in his heart that had been reaching out for something like a home ever since he arrived. Roxy was good and dear, but she wasn't his mother, and there was an emptiness in his own home with mother gone. He watched wistfully the companionship between this mother and daughter. It warmed his heart to know there was still such a mother and such a daughter.

So with a generous basket of lunch, they started off to the woods. April it was, but a warm sunny day, and the birds were singing all about, through the meadow, and trilling through the air, as if they were just crazy-happy at the return of spring. As if they were glad this soldier was home too, and this girl and he were going off to their out-of-doors to be happy together.

They climbed the hill over the meadow, enjoying every step of the way, and when they came to a fence they climbed it and went on, Barney catching Margaret's hand as they swung along together in the sunshine, like two children. Barney hadn't been so happy since his mother died. Somehow it had seemed to him those first few hours that he never would be happy again. That perhaps when people grew up they never were happy. Though when he thought back he realized that his own mother and father had been very happy together, and even after his father died his mother and he had always had glad times together, until the war came along and separated them.

They sat down on a mossy slope at last when they reached the top of the hill. It was warm and dry with the sunshine all the morning, and they were glad to rest.

"I wonder what's in that basket," said Barney, eyeing it wistfully. "I'm hungry, aren't you?"

Margaret smiled warmly.

"Wild strawberry tarts for one thing, I think. Mother made some yesterday. And there'll likely be chicken sandwiches. Are you as tired of chicken as everybody is these rationing days?"

"Me? Tired of *chicken?* Not on your life! We didn't always have all the chicken we could use over there in that hospital where I took my recovery. And I know your mother's chicken sandwiches will be something to boast about. And those dear little sharp pickles I just love. I think they must be peculiar to this part of the world for somehow I don't seem to remember having them anywhere else."

Just little nothings they talked about while they were eating, glad little nothings, that signified that they were happy to be together and having a grand time. And when they had finished everything in the basket, and drank the milk from the thermos bottle, they shook out the napkins, and closed the basket and settled down for a good talk.

"Now," said Barney, "we've got to get acquainted. You see you are not at all the same little child you were when I went away, and we have a lot to catch up on. You begin first and tell me all about you."

So Sunny told, pleasant little sketches from her sweet young life, and Barney watched her, impressing her lovely face like a picture on his heart. This was a girl worth cultivating. This was a girl in a thousand.

She told about the finish of her school days, about her brief year at college, before she was called home to teach. About her father and mother and the little intimate things of the farm life. She told of her school, and then of her Sunday school class, and the church choir and how she was having to play the organ because the man who used to play it had to go to war.

"May I go to church with you tomorrow?" he asked suddenly, interrupting her story.

"Oh, *will* you? And would you be able to sing a solo?

Our soloist is gone into the Navy, and I don't know anyone else to get on such short notice."

"Why, yes, I'll do my best, if you want me, but I'm really not much on singing any more. I've been in a war you know, and then in a hospital, and my voice is all shot to pieces. But I'll try."

Then he suddenly reached out and took her hand in his.

"You're cold," he charged. "I saw you shiver! Yes, I did. Your fingers are like little icicles." He took both her hands in his own and rubbed them softly.

"Such little bits of hands to do so many things," he said gently, looking down at them, smiling as if she was still the little child she used to be when he went away.

"Now come, we must walk around and get warm," he said suddenly. "In fact, I'm afraid it's time for me to go home. I've got some important letters to write and a phone call to make to Washington. But I've had such a nice time. May I come again?" Then he sprang up and drew her to her feet and they started on their way down the meadow.

It was on the way down the quiet meadow that Sunny suddenly looked up with a question.

"Do you have to go back to war, Barney?"

He gave her a quick glance and hesitated before he answered. Then he spoke earnestly.

"I sincerely hope so," he said. "I wouldn't have come away now if I could have had my way. But it seemed that at the time I had no strength to go on. I was just tired out. But now, the last few days, I feel rested, and I *want* to go back. I want to get this war done. That's what I'm telephoning to Washington about. That, and trying to find my friend Stormy. I've got a friend down there, an admiral, with a pretty big pull among the powers that be, and I'm going to see if I can't get them to send me back sooner than the stated time they gave me. I feel like a slacker staying home and resting day after day. It was wonderful at first, of course, hearing birds sing instead of bombs falling, getting the sound and smell of spring in a world that has not yet been desolated by war. And yet, since I've got around some and seen how little our people over here really understand what war is, I feel as if I must hurry back and do all I can. Oh, the people over here, some of them, many of them, think they know all about war because they can't have as much meat as they want, or coffee or shoes or sugar! They think thay are winning the war because they take a little time out of amusing themselves to entertain soldiers waiting to be sent over-seas, or to roll a few bandages occasionally in the Red Cross. If you had stayed with us last night and heard them talk you would have understood what I mean."

"I know," said the girl earnestly. "I don't wonder you feel that way. But I'm sorry you feel you must go back so soon. It's been so great to have you home again. And it does seem as if you really ought to stay until the doctor thinks it is right for you to return, if you must go. Of course, I understand how you must feel to be taken out of it before it is over, but it doesn't seem as if it was right that you should be allowed to go back into such strenuous action until you've really got rested. I should think they would insist on your taking your full leave."

"Perhaps they will," said Barney with a sigh, "but I'm hoping they'll see it the way I do. You see I have a reason. I have a buddy out there somewhere, perhaps among the enemy, who saved my life once when I was near to death. He was wounded himself, and had been doing hard duty for hours, and he came across me wounded, unconscious, in the dark, and strung me across his big splendid shoulders, even though he was badly wounded himself, and carried me back to my outfit. He carried me through enemy fire safely. I owe him my life. And now he is missing in action himself somewhere, or was when I came away, and I can't get him out of my mind. It may be he has been heard from, but I doubt it. They had about given up hope for him when I was sent home. But I've got it on my heart that I want to get permission to go back and hunt for him, save him from whatever mess he's in, if I can. I owe him that. He did as much for me, and after all he's a valuable man. He's done a lot in his special line. It may be I can make them see it my way."

"But—aren't *you* a valuable man too?" asked Sunny shyly.

"I wouldn't say so," smiled Barney, "not in comparison with Stormy Applegate. And what's my life if I can't give it for one who would have done the same for me?"

"I see," said the girl with sweet understanding in her eyes. "It's beautiful of you. And I can see why you want to go. Will they let you, do you think?"

"I'm not sure. I'm going to do my best to make them see it my way. But there's always a lot of delay and red tape about changes of this sort. I'm glad you can understand. It's nice to have a real friend. One who is in sympathy and can see why I must go, and soon, if I can get the chance."

"Yes," said the girl gravely, "I can see. But I could wish it didn't have to be."

With a tender understanding smile he took her hand in a quick grateful clasp.

"Thank you," he said, looking down at her gravely, "I'll remember that. It will help me. And you'll be praying, won't you?"

"Oh yes," said Sunny. "I've been doing that for you all the way through."

They had come to the highway. He helped her across the fence, took her up to the house, and then hurried home, and to the telephone.

10

MEANTIME the gang that had swarmed down upon him with a surprise party the night before had no intention of letting Barney get out of their clutches. They promptly organized their forces, and inaugurated a series of parties and dinners, calculated not only to keep his time rather full, but with the object in view of changing his whole point of view. They felt it was for his good that they should instruct him in the ways of this new and present world that war had brought to his home town. He simply must not be allowed to go around acting "pious" as they called it, just because he was in the old town where his mother brought him up that way.

To that end the gang took their way to the Vance home early on Sunday evening, carrying with them several large boxes of candy, feeling that this offering certainly would not start any antagonism, and could be passed around so casually that all would go smoothly.

The plan was to bring invitations to various parties, gatherings, and entertainments. They called themselves "The Community Cheer Association." Their professed object was to bring a degree of comfort and cheer to lonely mothers and wives and sweethearts of soldiers who were far away in peril on land or sea or air. The statement had been drawn up by Hortense, and she was clever at that sort of thing. There was ample opportunity for eloquence, and Hortense felt that if she knew anything at all about Barney Vance such an object would appeal to him at once, for she could see that Barney was still keen about his mother, so perhaps that would be the best appeal for a start. Later, when sentiment failed, a more worldly appeal would surely have a better chance. Of course Hortense did not tell all her satellites this. They thought they were merely assisting in a clever plan to divert Barney from a war obsession that threatened to make him prematurely grave and depressed, and they entered into the scheme with all their giddy young hearts. That is, all of them who were not already pledged to some defense outfit and about to leave for their assignments.

The Association arrived at the Vance home in the early gloaming while the church bells were still ringing far and near, and, a few birds were still chirping anxiously about the problems of the next day, involving the cat that had taken up a sniper's position behind the lilac bush and menaced every crumb that fell outside the kitchen door.

Roxy and Joel were sitting in the big rockers on the front porch enjoying the lovely night, for the moon was rising and there were many stars in sight. It wasn't often they got to enjoy a Sunday night rest on the porch, for they were regular attendants at church and never stayed at home for trifles. But Joel had stepped on a nail and had a very sore foot, so they had decided they ought to stay at home that night.

But when those noisy girls and boys drew up in the

driveway by the end of the front porch, Joel groaned aloud.

"There come those termagants again," he said angrily, and began to swing his sick foot down from the pillow on the chair that Roxy had arranged so comfortably for him. "It seems we're not to have any peace any more. Get your duds on, Roxy. I'm going to church!"

"No!" said Roxy sharply. "Sit still. Don't take your foot down! You're not going to church and neither am I. Leave this to me. I'll settle this thing."

Roxy got up and walked to the end of the porch, her hands folded neatly over the stomach of her Sunday dress.

"Yes?" she said in her most severe formal tone. "Did you want something?"

"We sure did," said Hortense defiantly. "We want Barney. Call Barney, won't you, right away? We've come to see him."

"Sorry," said Roxy loftily. "He isn't here!" She told herself in her heart that that wasn't quite true. She *wasn't* sorry. She was *glad* that Barney wasn't there. But she had been hearing the young people talk so much that that word "Sorry" had become common parlance, like a formal apology. Well, perhaps it was allowable in that sense. Then she called back her attention to what the hated Hortense was saying.

"Not here? Where is he?" she demanded.

"He didn't say where he was going," said Roxy severely.

"Well, when is he coming back?" she asked imperiously.

"Well, I wouldn't be able to say," said Roxy affably. "He doesn't consult me about his plans. He comes and goes as he wants to, you know."

Hortense gave her an unbelieving look.

"Well, that's ridiculous!" said the girl, curling her lip. "You probably know all about it. You're his old nurse and you always used to snoop around and find out. I'm sure you know perfectly well. So spill it out! We're in a hurry!"

Roxy stood there, her arms folded, looking at Hortense calmly. At last she asked:

"Would you like to leave a message?"

The other girls looked at their leader thoughtfully. Where would such a course get them?

But Hortense closed her lips firmly and shook her head:

"No," she said. "We wish to talk with Barney himself. We don't want any of your twisted reports carried back to him. Maybe we'll come in and wait for him. We could sing. We've got somebody here who can play for dancing. We could have a little dance and just wait for Barney to come back." She looked at them all for their assent.

"No!" said Roxy firmly. "You won't do that! This is Sunday and we don't have things like that going on in this house on Sunday."

"Well, this doesn't happen to be your house," said Hortense haughtily. "You really have nothing to say about it."

"It happens that we are in charge," said old Joel suddenly, hobbling over to the end of the porch, his voice gruff and dictatorial: "We're in charge of this house," he repeated firmly, and the young would-be guests looked at him in amazement. In all the years they had been coming to this house Joel had never put forth such a determined personality. He really looked threatening, standing there with one stocking foot wrapped about with bandages.

"Aw, c'mon Hortie," said Hank scowling at the girl

whose willing henchman he usually was glad to be. He well remembered a vigorous spanking administered in his youth by Joel after he was found picking raspberries from the Vance bushes.

"Yes, c'mon," echoed the girls. "Let's drive around a little while and see if we won't meet Barney."

"Yes, c'mon, Hortie," said Cap uneasily. "It's a nice night to drive around, and we don't wanta have an argument with that old guy. He looks unpleasant. I'd sorta hate ta have ta knock him out. C'mon, we can come back after a while!"

And suddenly Hortense decided he was right. Clamorously they drove away, shouting appropriate remarks to the old couple who had so effectually foiled their plans.

When they were out of sight in the moonlight, and out of sound down the road, Joel hobbled back and stood looking down at the chair where he had sat so comfortably a few minutes ago.

"That's what we got for staying home from church, Roxy," he remarked grimly. "If it wasn't so late I'd go yet. But seeing it *is* late and everybody would turn around and watch us hobble into the back seat in the middle of the sermon, suppose we go to bed, Roxy. I hate to give up sitting out here in the moonlight, but I can't stand having that gang coming back here, for I just know if they did come back I'd go out in spite of this ding-busted foot and wallop each one of them. I swear I would."

Roxy set her lips firmly and said, "Yes, let's go to bed. We'll lock all the doors, and turn out all the lights and then they can go hang. Barney has his key. And anyways, wherever he is, he *may* be pretty late coming in."

"Yes? I thought they said he had to rest? Didn't he

have doctor's orders? He don't seem to be keeping any orders very well," said Joel.

"Well, I guess there isn't anything we can do about it, is there?" drawled Roxy indifferently.

"Seems like," assented Joel, climbing into bed with a gingerly care for his sick foot. "But then Barney always was a good boy. I don't fancy he'll do anything to really upset his health. I heard him say he was keen to get back to war, and the quicker he gets okay, the quicker he can go, more's the pity. Although I can't help being glad he wasn't home tonight when those banshees arrived. I wonder what his mother would have done if she'd been here when they arrived?"

"Well, I'm glad she wasn't for her sake, but I'm sure if she had been she would have had some gentle very natural way of stopping the things she didn't approve. She always could, even when Barney was a mere baby. She never let the neighbor-children's gang get ahead of her. And yet she was friendly with them all, and always spoke gently to them. That's a real lady for you. Always speak gentle, but never let wrong things go on. They all knew that when she was alive, and they never tried any of their high shines on her. If I don't miss my guess her son's got the same gift, and they'll presently find out. Not till then will they let him alone."

Meantime Barney had gone to see Sunny, late that afternoon, in answer to a telephone invitation from Mrs. Roselle to come to Sunday night supper, and so have time to run over his solo before they went to church, and Barney accepted the invitation eagerly.

Ever since he had left Sunny at her home and hurried back to his unwritten letters, he had been thinking about her. Perhaps it was not conscious thinking, but nevertheless in the back of his mind her face had been hovering, and when he was reminded of her, of anything she said, of the way she looked when she said it, there was a kind of satisfaction in his mind about her. She had grown up just as her sweet little child personality had promised, and he was thankful that in the world there was one girl who was like that.

Barney had not been giving much thought to girls in the last two years. A few girls, friends of his college days, had written him several times each when he was overseas and in constant action, and he had answered them gaily as he had opportunity, and that had been the end of it. Some of the home young people had written occasionally, too, at first and then dropped out of his knowledge. And now he had come home and found to his disappointment that so many of them seemed to have changed, grown coarse, hard, giddy and selfish. He wondered if that could all be laid to the account of war and the changing world. And then when he spent a few hours with Sunny he had been so relieved to find that she was not like the rest.

So as he walked down the sunlit meadow that Sunday afternoon and up the hill toward her home he found his heart quickened with pleasant anticipation of going to meet one who had the same moral background as himself. The kind of living and thinking that had formed the background of home in his mind during those terrible days of war. The home to which he would go back, where living was sane, people had right ideas, men believed in God and at least tried to keep up a semblance of serving Him. He didn't think this all out in words, but it was a kind of atmosphere surrounding his thoughts and made him pleasant company on his walk in the sunshine.

So the afternoon had been a congenial one, exchanging thoughts with one who was in sympathy with the convictions he felt were most vital.

Sitting under the trees in the old rustic chairs where

he remembered sitting long ago when he had come over on some errand for his mother, they had a long talk. Only instead of the little girl, whose name was Sunny, who used to beg him to swing her, or to play ball with her, there was this slim lovely girl just as sweet-faced, with just as bright hair, who went by the name of Margaret. And she seemed to know all the answers to the questions he asked, and was deeply interested in every topic he introduced. She wanted to know about his thoughts and feelings when he went into battle. Things he had never expected to tell anyone, now that his mother was gone. But he found himself telling this girl his innermost experiences.

All too soon the delightful talk was over, as they were called to the pleasant dining room, and the delicious supper. Hot muffins and strawberry jam, hot chocolate with whipped cream. Tempting slices of cold chicken, crisp celery, a luscious maple-walnut cake, and canned peaches from the peach orchard back of the house.

Then suddenly it was getting late. There was scarcely time to go over the solo before they started for church.

"You know I really haven't any business singing a solo," said Barney as he folded up his music.

"Why not, I should like to know?" asked Margaret. "Your voice is even better than I remember it, and I used to think it was the most wonderful voice I had ever heard."

"Oh, you were just a kid you know. But I really haven't done any singing for two years, except as a crowd of fellows always sing in their leisure time when they get together."

"Well, your voice is as good as ever," said the girl earnestly," and *I* know. I really do. We had a very noted singer staying in the neighborhood all last summer, and he used to ask me to play his accompaniments sometimes. I used to think his voice was like yours. It was very beautiful."

"You're very flattering," smiled Barney, "but I'm afraid you're prejudiced. And I do hope you will not be disillusioned about my voice when I sing tonight."

"No," said Margaret, "I'm sure I shall not. I am entirely satisfied at the way you have just been singing. Now, let's forget it. I don't want you to get self-conscious. Look at that sunset. Isn't it glorious? It makes my heart thrill the way it thrilled me while you were singing,

And the glory, the glory of the Lord, shall be revealed,
And all flesh shall see it together."

"It's rather presumptive in me to attempt such a big thing when I'm practically off a battlefield and a hospital bed."

"Never mind. You're not to think of that. Remember your audience has not been hearing many oratorios and masterpieces of music, and it will be the words that you will get across to them. Certainly you can put over words with music better than anyone I ever heard."

They walked slowly down the road together into the glory of the evening, as the sunset lit their way. It seemed to them both that it was the end of one of those perfect days that only come now and then, like resting places on the way to Heaven.

Mercifully they were spared meeting that cavalcade of would-be callers who had come out searching for Barney, for they had gone in the opposite direction, and there was nothing to spoil the beauty of their walk to church, with the church bells ringing out in the sweet air, now near, now far, and now and again a sleepy bird giving a flutelike call, and with happiness in their hearts.

Then they were at the church, his mother's church, and all the old friends sitting in their accustomed seats, some of them—sweet old faces, his mother's friends, old men and old women, carrying on at home, very few younger men in the audience, just a few in uniform. He could recognize the grin on a few of those uniformed young faces. They had been little boys sitting around the sidelines when he was playing baseball.

The old minister in the pulpit, with a kindly voice that trembled a little and white hair that had grown scant, was the same minister who had been in the pulpit for years. He had been retired, and the pulpit had been filled by a younger man. But he had gone into the service as a chaplain, and the old minister was back carrying on. Barney was glad of that. It seemed more natural with old Mr. Copeland there. He gave a tender glance toward the old-fashioned pew where his mother used to sit, and where for years he had sat beside her, finding the hymns for her, and the place in the Bible; and looking over with her.

Barney had taken a retired seat in the choir, at one side of the organ, most of the choir in front of him, and he had the advantage of being able to see everybody in the house, without himself being conspicuous. Also, when the young organist took her place at the organ he found himself where he could watch her sweet face with its earnest changing expression. It gave him opportunity to study her without seeming to stare. He was glad to find her face just as flawless, just as sweet and unworldly at such close range as he had judged it to be when he was talking with her, across the room, and he continued to be amazed that she, so young in a world at war, had been able to mature so beautifully, and without the hardness of so many of the current age.

Then he grew interested in the music, and marveled

that she played so well. Not that he was a connoisseur in music, though during his college days he had managed to hear some of the best, and to enjoy it greatly.

When it came time for his solo he found himself so in tune with the whole sweet simple service that he felt none of the reluctance to sing that he had had when Sunny first asked him. He let the song roll forth with its message, till the audience hushed into breathlessness, listening. And there were tears even in some old eyes as the listeners remembered Barney's mother, wondering if in Heaven she could know, and hear.

Some of his old playmates, who had been deferred because of some physical ailment, sat in wonder at him, and drank in the message of his song as something they seemed to have missed out on so far. For Barney sang as if the words of his song had taken deep hold upon his life, and he were urging them to accept what he had. There was one fellow, Cy Baxter by name, a little older than Barney, who had been morbid for months because he couldn't get in anywhere, army or navy, and had to stay quietly in the bank and be looked down upon by the others as a slacker. The bank was all right of course in peacetime but it made him feel like an old man now, and all because of a little physical defect.

But when he heard Barney singing he caught some message from that song that pointed his heart above. Somehow Barney got it across to him that God wanted him right where he was, and because it had been ordered by God that was the highest honor he could have had. Afterward he wondered what it was, what had been the words Barney had sung that had made him willing to yield to God's will and do what he was doing with a smiling face and a satisfied soul, even if he would have been so much better pleased if he might have gone out and done some of the brave hazardous deeds that Barney was reported to have done.

Did the angels somehow convey the message to Barney that he was not just entertaining old friends and neighbors who were curious about him for his mother's sake, but that he was singing to souls who needed a message? For that was the way he sang. And to his own astonishment, that was the way he felt.

It seemed, when the benediction was pronounced, that it had been a blessed service and he was glad he had gone.

Afterwards, they swarmed around him and thanked him, those old friends of his childhood, friends of his mother's, and some few who remembered his father. They told him how much they had enjoyed his singing, and how proud they were of all he had done in the service, and proud that afterward he had cared enough to come back to the old church. And Cy Baxter had lingered indifferently in the back of the church until most of the others were gone, and then he came up and gripped Barney's hand and said fervently: "Say, Barn, that was *swell!*" Barney looked in his eyes, saw a hint of tears, and gripped Cy's hand warmly.

"Thanks, pard!" he said. "Glad you liked it." But there was a message warmer than just those words in Barney's eyes, almost tears behind his own glance, as his hands held the other young man's hand with a lingering pressure. Somehow, there seemed to be a bond forged right there that linked a chain to Heaven.

The young organist's cheeks were rosy as she watched the reaction to Barney's song, and she was more pleased than at any praise that had ever been given to her.

It was on the way home that she told him how his singing had stirred her, and how she had seen the effect on different ones in the audience.

"Oh, Barney!" she said. "I wish you were going to stay here and help in that choir! Of course I know that's not to be compared with the work you are doing in service for the country, but oh, I believe you could reach *souls* with your voice!"

"Thank you, Margaret," he said, laying his hand for an instant on the little hand that rested on his arm. "I had never thought of that as a calling, but I'd be glad if I might help people sometimes that way."

They were walking slowly, too much stirred by the service, and the warm reception of the people, to be willing to have it over soon.

Then suddenly the girl looked up.

"How did you make out with your Washington call yesterday, Barney?"

"Oh, Washington. Yes. Why, I found my man, the admiral, was out of the city. I'm to see him at eleven o'clock tomorrow."

"Oh," she said with a tight little catch in her breath. "Well—I'll be praying for you."

"Thank you," he said, "I'll be remembering that," and he laid his hand on hers again with another quick pressure. "But," he said, after a minute, looking down at her almost mischievously, "which way will you be praying? That I'm to go, or stay?"

Margaret was still for a minute and then she looked up confidently and answered:

"I'll be praying for *God's* way."

"That's great!" said Barney thoughtfully. "That puts it up to God, doesn't it? And after all I wouldn't want it otherwise. I don't want to impose my wishes in this. I'll make my offer to Washington, but I can't really do anything else about it but that. God knows where Stormy is, and if He needs me to go after him. I'll just ask Him too, to take over, and have it His way. Thank you for making me see that."

Walking home alone in the moonlight afterwards, he thought again what an unusual girl Sunny had developed into, and rejoiced. He was glad he had come home to get to know her again as she was now. What a girl to have for a friend!

ROXY, wearing an old dressing gown that had done duty almost ever since she had been in service, and her front hair in curlers, appeared at the door with a speck of a flashlight in her hand while Barney was trying to find the keyhole.

"Oh, is that you, Roxy?" he said, somewhat startled to find the house in darkness. "What's the matter? Something gone wrong with the electricity?"

"No," said Roxy ruefully, "it's just that we've had callers, and they said as how they might be coming back when you got home. They said it was important they see you tonight."

Barney slid inside the door, shut it firmly, and locked it before he spoke. Then he stood with his back against it and said:

"Who was it, Roxy? Not that gang again?"

"Yes, the very same. Joel and I were sitting on the front porch and I had his bad foot all fixed comfortable on a cushion, and we was enjoying the moonlight, when they come roistering into the drive and ordered me to call you. And when I said you weren't here they wanted to know where you was, and I said you hadn't told me. And they wanted to know when you'd be back, and I said I hadn't any idea. And first they was going to come in and play the pianna and dance, but Joel he got up and ordered them out. I never saw Joel so riled up, not before folks. They tole him this wasn't his house, but he said he was in charge of it, and they hadta *go*. He said it was Sunday night and we didn't have such goings on here Sunday night. So they decided to go, but they said they'd drive around and find you, and they'd come back later. And I wouldn't put it past 'em to come, no matter how late it was, so Joel and I locked all the doors and turned out the lights and went to bed. We thought that might discourage 'em a little if they found it dark. But now you've come, if you want the light you do as you please. You could hang some blankets over your windows if you want to sit up and read or anything, but I thought I'd wait and tell you."

"No, of course not, Roxy. I can get to bed in the dark. I've done it many a time in my life, especially since I've been in service. I'm sorry I kept you up so late, but I certainly don't want a visitation tonight again. Can you find your way with that flashlight? All right, I'll come up behind you. Is this all the doors to lock? Okay. I think they'll be disappointed if they come back again tonight. No, I don't need the flashlight. I know every inch of this house from garret to cellar, dark or light. Don't worry about me. Wasn't I born and brought up in this house? There, find your way to bed, Roxy. Good night!" and Barney went to his own room, took off his shoes, and lost no time in getting undressed and into bed. He was sound asleep when the gang returned, and drove up to the house.

He might have heard them discussing whether he had come home yet, if he had been awake, but he was tired after the pleasurable excitement of the day and evening, and he always slept soundly, so he did not waken. But Roxy, over on her side of the house was crouching down by the window sill and she heard them.

"He probably hasn't come home yet," said Hortense. "Soldiers generally stay out late when they go to see a girl. I wonder who she is? I wonder if he took the train or not?"

"Aw, you forgot he's under orders and s'posed to go to bed at a certain time, don't you remember?" drawled Hank. It was evident that he had no relish for another encounter with Joel. He remembered that Joel wielded a heavy hand, and Hank was no fighter.

"Oh you poor simp, didn't you know that that talk about orders and rest was all bunk?" said Hortense. "You don't catch Barney Vance doing anything he doesn't want to do, not with his army orders several thousand miles away over a lot of ocean. What I'm aiming to do is to make Barney *want* to break orders, and do what *we* want him to do, and I mean to win out, too! Well, let's drive around a little more, and come back past here again, to see if there's any light. It isn't midnight yet."

"Mebbe he's gone down to Washington," volunteered Amelia. "I heard him say he might have to go down pretty soon to report to some doctor or something."

"Well, if that's the case we might meet the midnight train and bring him home. How about it, Hank? Drive over to the highway and let's meet the Washington train. The local one, too. He may have been visiting some friend of his mother's, or some girl he met somewhere. But we can't afford to let too much time go by before we get our plans started."

So with much hilarity they drove away again, and

Roxy crept thankfully into her bed, hoping the home-enemy was subdued for the night at least.

But Barney was sound asleep, dreaming of Stormy Applegate who had saved his life.

And over in another white farm house about a mile or so away, where the lights were out and the family slept, the girl that used to be little Sunny, knelt beside her bed and prayed earnestly that such things as she desired might go God's way. And afterward when she lay down to rest, her heart kept thrilling over the notes that Barney Vance had sung in church that night, and she went to sleep praying: "Oh, God, bless Barney Vance, and make him into what You want him to be. And oh, take care of him, for Your name's sake."

The next morning's mail brought a number of letters for Barney, and among them were several invitations, for those girls had lost no time in getting their invitations into the early morning mail.

Barney opened two from overseas first, gay messages from his buddies who were still with the company, one from a nurse in the hospital where he had been recuperating, enclosing one of his handkerchiefs he had left behind him. He was glad to get that for it was the last little thing his mother had sent him, and he prized it very highly. He had left it under his pillow in the hospital, and she had found it when she put fresh linen on the bed.

She was a nice little nurse, and had served him well. It was kind of her to take so much trouble for him. He would have to write and thank her, of course.

Then he came to the three little notes. The first one from Amelia, asking him to come over prepared to stay the evening and take dinner with her family. She said they wanted to hear all about his experiences in the war. He frowned, flung down the letter and picked up the next. That was from Lucy Anne Salter. She was inviting him to take lunch with her and her mother on Tuesday noon, and divulging cleverly that she had borrowed her grandmother's car for the afternoon and they were going to take a drive over to the neighboring navy camp that wasn't too far away. They would return in time for dinner at the inn and see a movie for the close of the evening.

Barney tossed the letter after the other one and began to laugh.

"What is this, Roxy, a conspiracy? Or is it a social club? Wait! Here's another! From Martha and Madge Wrexall, as I live! They want me for an all-day picnic at Hunter's Park, dancing in the evening in the pavilion. Special war music for the soldiers! Can you beat it, Roxy? What do they think I am? Why a *strong* man couldn't stand all that program, and here I am *invalided* home!"

Roxy sat grimly disapproving with anxiety written across her loving face.

"I could tell we weren't done with that crowd yet," she said with a sigh. "What are you going to do, lad? You couldn't stand all that froth. I could tell by your eyes after their first raid on you. You better take to your bed for awhile and let me tell them you are sick."

"Not on your life, Roxy! Let that gang drive me to bed? Not if the court knows itself, and she thinks she does. No, I'll just write a nice little note to each one and tell them I'm having to run down to Washington on business, and when I get back I shall be much too busy to accept social engagements. How will that do? Of course I hate to hurt some of those people, but I just can't take it. They aren't my kind, Roxy."

"I should say not," said Roxy indignantly. "But they think just because you wear a uniform you ought to be willing to go the whole way and have a regular riot-act while you're here."

"Well, they'll find out they're mistaken," said Barney striding over to his mother's desk and opening a drawer where he knew she always kept writing paper.

He sat for a few minutes scratching away with his fountain pen, and presently presented Roxy with appropriate answers declining all his invitations.

"There! See how they sound will you? And then will you kindly give them to the postman when he comes, so he can get them around before the evening? Especially that one for tonight, Amelia's. And meantime I'm taking the train right now for Washington, see? You don't know how long I have to stay. Tell them I have an appointment with an admiral down there, and I'm not sure when I shall get back, so you can't make any promises for me. I shall be very busy when I come. Maybe by and by I'll have a party myself, and invite them all, but if I do I'll set the program my way, and I don't mean maybe. See?"

"Yes, I see," said Roxy with a troubled look. "And I'll do my best, even if Joel and I have to go to bed to get rid of them. But boy, there's something else. This morning Mrs. Kimberly telephoned that she was having a guest some day this week who was going to stay a few days with her, her niece, Cornelia Mayberry, and she was crazy to see you. She said her brother was overseas with you and he had written her to come on and get acquainted with you. Now what shall I say to her? I told her I'd tell you and I thought you'd be glad to see her sometime, but now I better tell her you're going away and not say anything more about it, hadn't I?"

Barney looked up startled.

"What do you say her name is? Mayberry? Cornelia Mayberry? Why sure, I'll *have* to see her. Her brother was one of my closest buddies through all our engagements over there. He used to talk a lot about her. He thought she was tops. You fix it up, can't you Roxy? Just because I don't want to go carousing around with that other gang is no sign I can't have any friends. And anyway, they don't need to know everything I do. You know how to be polite and get out of things, I know, Roxy, because you always sent the people home that mother didn't want here without making them mad either. You'd give them each a cooky or something, and they never got mad."

"Of course," said Roxy with a smile.

Then suddenly Barney looked at his watch, and sprang to his feet. "For Pete's sake! I'm gonta miss my train if I don't hurry. Bye, Roxy! Be a good girl, and don't worry about me if I don't come back right away. I'll be all right, and you know I *have* to stay as long as they say."

Then Barney went striding down the road at a good military pace, arrived at the station just two minutes before the train came in, and missed by half a second a contact with two of his would-be hostesses. He saw them from the car window and hid behind his morning paper so they wouldn't see him. In the name of all conscience, why did girls want to make such fools of themselves? Running after a fellow until he wished he had never seen them. Not even giving him a chance to look them over and see if he liked them yet. Then he fell to wondering what Cornelia Mayberry would be like. Would she resemble her brother? He was a good guy, and he was crazy about his sister. He would just have to show her a little attention. How would she fit with Margaret Roselle? Would Margaret like her?

And there was another question. If it turned out that Miss Mayberry was to be in town long and he would be expected to pay her a little attention, what other fellows and girls could he get together? There was Sunny, of course, in case she would be willing to help him, but what fellows were home whom he could call upon? If only Stormy were here he would jump right in and help. Stormy was that way. Good old Stormy! Would he ever see him again?

And then his thoughts merged into a plan for what he would say to the admiral in case he succeeded in seeing him. Oh, if he could only be allowed to go and hunt for Stormy! At least to make sure if he was dead or alive. Praise God he was in Heaven if he had died, but if he was still alive, if only he might rescue him somehow from any unpleasant experience he might be undergoing!

Back in his home town of Farmdale a little school teacher with bright hair and earnest eyes was praying for him, all day long. Always in between what she was doing she was crying out in her heart to God to keep him, and to help him to get his friend back if he was still in need of help.

Barney sat for awhile staring out the window, scarcely seeing the quick rushing landscape, thinking what it would probably be like when the war was finally over, and the boys came back. What it would be like to have Stormy living over here perhaps. He remembered that Stormy had once said longingly that he wished he could go back home to America and live an old-fashioned normal life again. Good old Stormy! Would that ever be? Or had he already begun a heavenly life?

Then suddenly he noticed that the train was coming into Washington. There was the dome of the Capital, the sharp point of the monument, and the distant out-lines of the lovely Lincoln Memorial. He would be in time to see the cherry blossoms. He had seen them once, long ago, when he was a boy in high school and went with the high school crowd on that memorable trip to see his nation's capitol.

He caught up his bag and hurried out. Would his admiral have arrived yet? Would he be able to see him today, or would there be a lot of tiresome waiting around, and then more waiting, and then maybe disappointment at last?

Meantime, back at his home in Farmdale, Roxy was having troubles of her own. She simply couldn't get any work at all done because she was continually being called to the telephone.

Amelia, first, in great dismay.

"Roxy, isn't Barney there? Won't you let me speak to him right away? He hasn't gone anywhere *yet,* has he?"

"Yes, Miss Amelia," answered Roxy pleasantly. "He went on the early train this morning."

"Oh, do you mean he's just gone to the *city?*"

"No, Miss Amelia, he's gone to Washington." There was satisfaction in Roxy's tone as she announced this importantly.

"To *Washington!* My goodness! I thought he was invalided home and had to rest. Did he go sight-seeing? I shouldn't think that was very restful."

"No, Miss Amelia, I'm sure he's not gone sight-seeing. I think he was under some sort of orders. You know he has to report to the government from time to time." Roxy didn't know this. She merely *assumed* it. She thought it would make her answers have more weight if they seemed to be official.

"Well, but—isn't he coming back *tonight?*"

"He didn't know when he would be back. He took a suitcase with him."

"Oh, for Pete's sake!" exclaimed the dismayed Amelia. "I was having a party especially for him tonight, and I've got all the other people invited."

"That's too bad," said Roxy sympathetically, "but he wouldn't want you to stop on that. He said something about some invitations, but I thought he wrote notes to explain why he couldn't be there."

"Yes, I got a note, but I thought if he was coming back tonight I'd just tell him to come over anyway, no matter how late he was."

"Yes?" said Roxy. "That's kind of you. But I don't think he is likely to come tonight. If he comes of course I'll tell him, but I don't think he's expected to be back tonight."

"Oh, how perfectly *horrid!*" said Amelia. "We certainly are having bad luck with Barney."

"Well, you can't count on service men you know, these war times," said Roxy sympathetically. "The government isn't thinking about parties when they give orders. You have to expect things like that."

"Mercy! You don't suppose they're going to send him back overseas right away, do you?"

"Well, I really wouldn't know," said Roxy serenely. "He hasn't said anything about it, but then perhaps he wouldn't know himself."

"Heavenly days!" said the disappointed Amelia. "What are we coming to? Life isn't really worth living any more, is it Roxy?"

"Well, that depends on what you think is really worth-while, I guess, doesn't it?"

"Worth-while?" queried Amelia bewilderedly, and suddenly hung up.

From then on all day Roxy was kept busy running to the telephone, always with a grin on her face. She really was enjoying this. It was one time when she had the situation well in hand and those "pesky young ones," as she called the young people, couldn't get the better of her.

And it wasn't only the young would-be hostesses of the week that did the calling up. Several of the rest of the young gang called up in dismay to verify the rumor that was going around that Barney might have been ordered overseas right away again. So Roxy quite enjoyed her day. It was a chance to make that crowd of good-for-nothings understand that they weren't the whole show in this world. She really was glad to see that crowd get their comeuppance once. The very idea of their getting up parties enough to fill Barney's whole time, when they knew he didn't hold with a lot of their wild goings on! Perhaps they couldn't understand that a person could keep his principles, even when he was off with a whole army who could do as they pleased about such little matters as principles.

But there was one girl who did not call up, and perhaps she was the one girl who had known that Barney was going away. But Roxy wasn't even sure of that, for Sunny Roselle was a very quiet mannered girl who didn't go around running after boyfriends, even if they had been friends from very long ago. And even if he had taken her to church, and sung a solo for her in the service! This bit of news she had learned from more than one of her loquacious telephone callers that day. They hadn't been there themselves, but others had told them about that song, and they were calling up to make sure it was true. But all they succeeded in doing was to make Roxy sorry she hadn't been present, and she and Joel had a little time of mourning over it that evening when they again sat on the porch to enjoy the twilight.

"He mighta told us about it," grumbled Joel.

"He *wouldn't*," said Roxy. "Did you ever hear him boast about anything yet?"

"Well, no, but Sunny mighta told us."

"She didn't have a chance," said Roxy. "Besides she probably thought we'd be at church."

"Yes, I s'pose so," mourned Joel.

"Well, we'll likely have other chances. They'll ask him again from all I hear, and if I don't miss my guess there'll be an increase in the attendance of young people at next Sunday night's service."

"Yes, if he ain't gone overseas by that time," mourned Joel. "Come on, let's go to bed. I gotta sow that south meadow in the morning, and I gotta get up early."

12

STORMY Applegate, escaped a pitifully short distance from the camp where he had been interned by the enemy for several weeks, half-starved and ill-treated, had found refuge in a broken shed in the rear of a decrepit dwelling that might have been at one time the remnants of someone's home. It was isolated and desolate now, with outlying buildings and occasional other remains of houses for several miles around, as a result of being in occupied territory.

Watching stealthily for some hours, Stormy decided there was no one anywhere near. He could not even see a lagging guard, so far was he from the surrounding fence of the camp.

Toward evening, hungry and thirsty, weak with long fasting, he ventured forth toward what was left of an old garden back of the house. He was sure he had sighted a sickly looking leaf that might mean a possible vegetable or two. Even a frozen leaf might be edible, sickly looking though it was. It might serve to still the awful gnawing in the region of his stomach, and enable him to keep on. Perhaps that woodland a mile or two away might shelter a stream where he could get water to hearten him for his adventurous journey.

The landscape was a blank desert. Not even a dog in sight. No birds even in the distance except a hovering hawk, circling, identifying prey from the sky, which might mean some prisoner had died and been cast forth for the elements to do their worst and save the trouble of burying him.

Stormy in his weak state shuddered, and crept forward cautiously. Even if one had been watching with binoculars from a distance he could scarcely have been seen to move, so slow and steady was his progress. He was so nearly the color of the earth about him, so burned with the sun and rain to which he had been continuously exposed, that he was practically invisible, a neutral that would never be noticed. At least he hoped that might be so.

Lying thus in the old garden ruts he found a few frozen roots that he could gnaw on. There was not much sustenance to be had from them, but at least it helped the awful craving for food.

When the shadows were growing longer on the wide sullen ground, and he was satisfied that there were no more roots to be found in that location, he crept on, keeping the old barn between himself and the camp from which he had come. And once he came to a sedgy place where tall grasses stood grimly in marshland, and when he went close enough he was able to reach down and wet a corner of his grimy rag of a handkerchief, his one remaining remnant of a civilized life.

He was so weak that he lay for sometime near this source of water, realizing that he ought to wash out that dirty handkerchief, for it might be a long time before he came near any water again, and to have one clean rag would be a comfort in all his squalor. But at last he roused himself and washed the rag as best he could, wiping his face with its wetness, licking his parched lips, washing the rag again and again, gaining new strength from the few drops of filthy water he was able to suck from the rag.

Dusk was coming down over the land again, and with it more comparative safety. He put his head down in the coolness among the tall grasses, and prayed.

"Oh God, I'm going on now. You said you would go with me. Show me where and how to move. I am still Yours, but I'm very tired and weak. Do with me what you will for Christ's sake. I'm Stormy, you know. Trusting to the end. Don't let me fall before the enemy."

Then he crept on.

As evening began to come down, and there were no lights whatever to be seen except very far ahead, and no sounds of a living human being, nor even animal, no birds' cries in the gray deserted sky, as if it were made of brass, Stormy steadied himself to his feet and managed to walk a few steps. It was a rest from the continual creeping and rolling he had been subjected to all day. But still he found he was very weary, for the weakness was growing upon him, and his hands and head felt hot. Was it fever coming on? Could it be poison from the stream where he had drunk? But no, there would have been no reason for even an enemy to poison a bit of sedge water so far from human habitation.

On and on he went, realizing that the night would be short at most for him to get away, counting up the mileage as he had calculated it, and what he had yet to go.

Now and again he would stretch himself for a moment on a bit of a grassy place, or where there was some dry moss, but he dared not go to sleep lest morning would steal upon him and find him no farther out of danger. He must get on as far as possible tonight.

As the night progressed and his weary footsteps lagged, he began to wonder if perhaps God meant him to die here, on the way, without ever a chance to get the information he had bought at such a price, back to his outfit. Was it all going to be of no avail? Had he taken this last trip for nothing after all? True, he had downed planes, he had done his part at driving the enemy back, but that needed information about conditions, that he had volunteered to get at all hazards, was still in his own mind. Even if he dared to write it, he would not dare to send it, here from an enemy-infested land. Here where every move of contact with his own world would be watched alertly, and worse than death would be the retaliation.

As he lay down midway between midnight and dawning, the dizziness overcame him so that he almost lost consciousness for a little moment, and then, his partly waking soul dazedly wondered if this was the end. The weakness and utter weariness seemed to submerge him again, strong man though he had been. Of course he had been for weeks on very short rations, and knew he was half starved, but strange visions began to swim across his rousing consciousness. A vision of a face—was that a girl he had seen sometime? Or could it be an angel come to conduct him Home? Was this then the end of his struggle? The end of his service to his country? Had he done all that God expected him to do in this great crisis?

The sweet face was smiling down at him. It seemed a girl who knew him. Was that what angels were like? Or if it were a girl, how did she get here, on the edge of a forest in a land he did not know?

As he came back to life again after that brief rest he tried to clear his mind and think. Her face was clearer now, and she was somehow connected with his company. Some member of his company. Who was it? Surely he could remember! Mayberry, that was the name. Lieutenant Mayberry's sister. She had visited her brother once at camp, and Mayberry had introduced her to him. A lovely girl! Gray eyes and dark hair, softly curled about her face. He looked again at the vision above him there in the edge of the forest. And now her name was coming. Cornelia! That was it. Cornelia Mayberry! A lovely name, and her brother had called her Cornie. She had a beautiful smile too. She had smiled at him when he said good night to her before she left on the evening train. He hadn't known her before that night, though he had seen her several times in the distance, and admired her, she seemed so unspoiled. He had seen her picture too in her brother's barracks. A face untarnished by the make-up of the world. She had made a deep impression upon him. Sometime when the war was over, if he came through alive, he would like to get to know a girl like that. That was what he had thought the night of the day he had met her, and then put the memory of her aside. Some day he might find a girl like that for himself. Would that ever happen? Or was he just dreaming of Heaven? "God, are You there? And is that vision one of Your angels, or was that Cornelia-girl come out of my heart to smile at me? Was it really that girl? And did You tell her to come? She doesn't belong to me, You know. Her people belong to the rich of the earth, and I'm just plain Stormy Applegate, but I'm Your child! Oh, God, is there something wrong with my head? Things seem so queer! Help me! Don't let me play out before I can get back and make my report."

It was almost dawn when he awoke again with a start. His head was clearer, but when he tried to sit up he was still very dizzy and he had to wait a few minutes before he dared to struggle to his feet again. Even then he had to grope ahead with his hands from tree to tree, almost ready to topple over. Unsteady from now on he was going to be, and yet he must go on as long as there was breath in his body. This was the job he had undertaken to do, and he must get back with his information or the whole expedition was a failure. He must not climax his life by failure at the end. If he could only find something edible.

Finally he heard the babbling of a little brook, and he slid down to his knees and drank deeply.

Somewhat refreshed he crept along through the rough ground of the woods, crawling on hands and knees, stopping now and again to lay his head down on his big dirty hands and close his eyes. It seemed to make it more possible for him to get a deeper breath again. If he could only get plenty of deep breaths he could go on.

But at last he came to the edge of the woods, and a wide lonely hillside stretched down before him. No gardens anywhere. Or was that a little patch farther on? He strained his eyes to see, and then struggled on. Finally, when a smooth stretch of hillside developed he lay down and tried his old trick of rolling. But when presently he came to a rise in the ground, that stopped his progress. Then he was quite dizzy again, and wondered how he was to go on, but lying still awhile he took a new lease on life and looked around carefully, searching for something green he might dare to eat. If only there were a stream that might have fish, yet how could he catch fish? No line, no hook. Only his bare hands, no longer strong enough to be deft, alert. If only there were hens somewhere that might leave an egg about in this stark land. If only there were a cow he could try to milk. But there seemed to be no living inhabitants in the few dilapidated houses that dotted the bleak landscape ahead of him.

It was growing dark again. If he only could walk, really walk, there was no reason why he couldn't make time now, with no danger of being seen.

The thought gave him a new spurt of courage. He drew a deep breath, and tried to pretend that he was only a few rods from his destination, although he well knew that was far from true.

It was more than the middle of the night when he came to a group of rough houses.

Cautiously he stole from one to the other, peering into the dusty windows, studying the closed doors. Somehow those houses looked uninhabited, yet he dared not presume. He was only thankful that his mind was still keen enough to realize that he must be careful. Yet he bungled on slowly, from one building to another, and at the very last one he found the door an inch ajar.

Carefully listening, peering into every side of the small sordid edifice, revealed no inhabitant.

With fear and trembling he ventured to shove the door wider open and look inside. Nobody about. Utter silence in the small dim precincts. He crept within and let his trembling hands feel his way. If he only had a match, or a flashlight, but he had been a long time away from such amenities. He began to feel his way again cautiously, slowly. It was evident that there were no householders here, for surely if there were he would at least hear the sound of breathing. His sensibilities seemed to have grown keener since he had entered a place with four walls. He must be very careful! If he could only find something to eat, or a drink of water! Would there perhaps be two dry sticks he could rub together to make a light? But no, he must not dare do that. There might be a dweller somewhere about, or approaching. They would see and come. Or the enemy might be hidden watching. There were so many things to be thought of on this strange journey.

Then his hand came into contact with a tin basin. He felt cautiously inside. Something was rolling around in there. Two smooth round objects. Eggs. They were eggs! Could that be true? Or were his senses deceiving him?

He was sure now that this little group of buildings must be a place from which the dwellers had departed in haste before the approach of the enemy. That might explain the open door. They had hurried away, and left those two eggs. How long ago? How old were those two eggs? Would even a rotten egg keep life in his body? He slipped them in the pockets of his ragged blouse, and moved on. He must not venture to stay here too long. The owner could be returning. After daylight he could tell more about things. What was that on the floor that his foot had touched? He stooped to feel. A pair of shoes, and a tin can, still unopened. There might be something eatable there. Then he came upon a few more cans, some on a shelf above his head, three on the floor as if dropped in a hurry. Surely this spoke of sudden flight. Wasn't that right reasoning?

He stuffed the cans inside his blouse, and groped on. There was a crude chair. He almost fell over it, and there was a garment of some kind lying across it. It felt like a coat. It had pockets. He deposited the next can he found in one of the pockets. Then it came to him that he was rifling somebody's house. But he had to do it to save his own life, if he would get away. His mission was important. He must not stop for anything. And if he lived he could some day come back and pay the man for what he had taken, provided he could find the man, and the place. Oh God, are You here?

The late moon was peeping over the rim of the world,

and suddenly looking into the high dusty window, revealing a clutter of other articles.

Now, if he could only find some water, or a can opener, or something that he might drink. He felt as if he could not stand up another second, and to lie down there, with perhaps the owner, or worse still the enemy, not far away, was certainly sure death.

He groped again and his hand came into touch with a pail half filled with water. He lifted a handful to his face, put his lips to it. Even the thought of it was refreshing.

Then suddenly, feeling back along the shelf above the water pail he found a tin box with three matches in it. Dared he light one? No, better not venture. He stepped over to the door. He must go. Far in the distance he heard a sound. He must get out and into shadow.

Outside the moon had slipped behind a cloud. It was heavily dark, and he had three matches, but he dared not use them. He crept on hurriedly, his heart palpitating until it almost choked him. It occurred to him that he was probably following those who had earlier found escape down this same path he was taking. Would he find them later, in case he was able to go on?

After a little he crept within a group of stunted bushes, back from the path he had been going, and tried one of the eggs, breaking the end open against a stone he found by the wayside. He smelled it. It wasn't bad. Not too bad. He was not in a condition to be squeamish anyway. And he sucked the eggs as if they were the very breath of life, as indeed they were to him. Then he dropped his head down on his arms and closed his eyes for a few minutes. He mustn't go to sleep. No, he must get away from here as soon as possible while it was still dark.

He opened his eyes and attempted to go on. He was lame and sore in every joint and sinew, but he felt new vigor from the eggs he had sucked, and now before he started out again he ventured to knock a hole in one of the cans he was carrying. What if it should be tomatoes, or some kind of fruit juice?

A sharp stone was not hard to find, another blunt one for a hammer, and soon he had a hole in the top of that can. He applied his nose and got the smell of tomato juice. He tipped up the can and drank, long deep quaffs of the life-giving liquid. It seemed to go through his starved veins, and to put new vigor into his faint heart. And after he had drunk the juice, he started on again.

Still a great empty country, no town or even distant visions of a town. What had those cabins been where he had found the cans? Were they hastily built to harbor refugees as the enemy came into the land, and then abandoned as the internment camp was placed so near them? It was as if he were looking back and trying to read the story of what had happened along that way.

But even with the refreshment he had found in the cabin, his limbs were still very shaky, and it did not seem to him he could go on any farther.

But the stars were coming out again, and reminded him that he must keep on while they would guide him where he wanted to go. So he compelled himself step by step, making scarcely any progress, yet persisting.

At last he dropped down. Just a minute. He *must* sleep a minute.

And so he slept, on and on, and the night grew old, and the dawn crept on stealthily.

The baying of a distant hound burst suddenly upon the air, and though it was very far away it startled the weary man into quick frenzy.

He sat up sharply. He looked around him, and up. The stars were gone. Clouds had obscured them. But the hound kept on, and he came to himself and his caution.

There was no time to stop to consider. He must get on.

So he struggled to his feet and straggled on.

Of the three cans he still had with him two of them were canned milk, and the third was another can of tomatoes. In the morning he drank a can of milk, and lay down in a shadowed place in the woods to sleep once more. When he woke again his hands and head were burning, and he was shivering as with an ague.

"H'm! Trying to get sick!" he murmured to himself. "Can't afford to do that. Got to get on while the getting is good. When is this blamed desert going to be done?"

But he blundered up and stumbled on, more because his body was accustomed to the motion perhaps, than because he quite knew what he was doing. Only with that one steady idea behind it all that he had a job to do, to get his information back to the right sources in spite of anything, live or die, before it was too late. The same spirit with which he would have fought if he had been out on the battlefield, obeying combat orders from his officer.

There came a time when he finally fell, stumbling over some root or stone of which his fagged senses had not warned him, and when he fell he lay still. Perhaps he had struck his head. He was never quite sure afterwards, and when he came to semi-consciousness and wondered where he was, and how much longer this thing was going on, all he could really think about was the terrible burning heat of his head and body. His hands were like red hot furnaces as he lifted them to touch his face. He still gave a passing thought to his job, but he had to do something about this awful heat of his body before he could go on. So he lay and slept again at odd intervals.

And the next he knew he opened his eyes in a little wooden shack, on a bed of pine boughs, and a gruff man with hair on his face was bending over him and giving him water to drink. He couldn't quite make out what this meant, for he didn't recognize the man as one of his own outfit, so he hadn't reached his destination yet.

"Oh God, are You there?" he cried out at intervals. "If You're still there it's all right with me."

But the man who was attending him said nothing. Perhaps he spoke a foreign tongue. The fever and the dim light made it impossible to tell of what nationality the man came. He seemed only present as a vague shadow, perhaps one of those angels God sent sometimes. Certainly there could be no relation between him and the girl whose face had haunted him earlier in his journey. But sometimes this attendant brought him water to drink, and at times there was broth. Queer broth. He wasn't sure what it tasted of, but its warmth in his stomach, and its filling quality brought a little relief from the gnawing pain that had gripped his vitals.

Once in the night he looked about him to try to identify something, but all was strange. Just a blank wooden wall. The semblance of a small window, a door beyond. There was a fitful fire burning on an infinitesimal hearth, and there was smoke in the room. He was cold, and he was hot, yet once the old man bathed his face with an ill-smelling rag, and that seemed to help, till he got to shivering again.

"Oh, God, are You going to take me Home now?" he cried out once, as if the old man were not there. "But couldn't I first go by way of my own outfit and give the message I went over the line for? They need it Lord. But You know that. And if I don't take it, and You want them to have it, You've other ways of getting it to them. I'll just stay here till You tell me what to do."

Weird talking for the old foreigner to hear.

The old man went out one day for several hours and Stormy thought he was deserted. But then he came back with some herbs, and began to brew a concoction on the hearth, using a tin can for a cooking vessel. Later he administered it, a vile bitter mixture, and the sick man drank it because he could not help himself. Then he slept again, and when he woke there was more of the bitter medicine to swallow, and he too weak to resist.

He had no means of measuring time. He had long ago sold his wrist watch to a fellow prisoner in return for a garment he needed. But as time went on he felt a decided change. Some of the heat in his body was gone, the chills had stopped. He could swallow the tasteless broth because it appeased the terrible emptiness. And then he became aware the old man was speaking to him in a foreign tongue. He wasn't just sure what nationality it was, but there were parts of words that conveyed a vague meaning, and as he roused to the world again, and his need to go on living became more urgent he began to try to utter words himself. He tried a number of tongues of which he knew a smattering, and at last struck a few words the old man seemed to understand. Simple, basic terms, but with feeble gestures he could ask for drink, and food.

As the hours passed they talked a good deal, these two, so strangely brought together. They talked each in his own tongue, and understood but little.

But now and again when the sick man would cry out to God and look above, the old man would seem to understand that he was praying and would pause, whatever he was doing, and stand, head bowed, his hands crossed upon his breast. And afterwards he would point up and jabber a lingo, of which now and then Stormy thought he could cipher out a bit of meaning. He concluded at last that it was some queer dialect the man spoke, but his brain was too tired to try to figure out what it was. So with a method of his own, pointing to an object and saying a word over and over he managed to make the other man understand a few primitive ideas.

He had lost all sense of time, but one morning he woke, knowing he must get up that day, and must go on as soon as possible.

The old man looked sad when he pointed that he must go, and shook his head, but the next morning they separated. He could not make the old man go with him. He gathered from their meager communication that he was waiting for someone to come for him, and must not go away till his friend came.

So, with a bit of hard bread in his blouse and his one remaining can of condensed milk he started out alone, both pointing up, and waving quiet hands. After he had thanked his old nurse with a warm grasp of his hand, he started off down a hill in a softly gray morning, before the sun had quite decided what to do about shining that day, and now Stormy was out on his own, a little rested from his hours on the resinous bed of pine boughs, and much weakened by the fever that had taken its toll from his already weakened system.

He knew when he started that he would not be able to go far, and he must stop and rest shortly, but before he turned into a woodland stretch where there would be hiding, he turned and looked back and saw the dim figure of the old man standing where he had left him in the gray of the morning. So he lifted up his hand and pointed to Heaven and the old man lifted his arm and looked up.

"Oh God, You take care of him, and keep him safely till his folks come, please. This is Stormy asking, for Christ's sake."

The old man must have understood that he was praying for him for when Stormy looked back he saw the old man still standing with bowed head and hands crossed on his breast.

13

HOW frantic Barney Vance would have been if he could have known that even as he took the elevator up to the office where he was hoping to meet his friend the admiral in behalf of a scheme to find Stormy Applegate, that Stormy at that very moment was toiling, weary and footsore, and nigh unto despair along an unknown way. For Stormy was entering the first smart-looking village he had seen on his journeying from the detention camp, and he had just seen signs that it was enemy-occupied.

But Barney had thought so long about this desire of his to find Stormy that it had come to seem almost a dream, that might take years to accomplish. It was something he was working out to satisfy his own desire, and which everybody else seemed to think was utterly foolish and not worth the attempt, because they felt that Stormy was out of the running. He was either dead, or so hopelessly a prisoner that no one but God could save him, and Barney met so few in his questionings that even counted on God to do anything about such things that sometimes he questioned whether he might not be losing some of his own faith too. But still he felt he must make some attempt. If he found the admiral inclined to take this discouraging attitude and say it was out of the question, he didn't know what other earthly help he could try for. Perhaps it was all wishful thinking, this belief of his that Stormy was still alive. Perhaps he was just being foolishly sentimental, as several men and more than one girl had already told him frankly. Well, time would tell.

"Oh God," he prayed in his heart, "won't You work this thing out for me? This is the only thing I know to do. If it fails I won't know what to do next. I'll just have to let it rest with You. But please, if that's the way You want it, if I should make no further effort, please make me know somehow. Help me to be rid of this tormenting urge to go after him."

Then the elevator stopped at the floor he had named, and he got out and walked down the corridor to the door where he had been told to find the admiral.

And back in the schoolhouse where she presided over a restless throng of various-aged children, a golden-haired girl was earnestly praying in her heart as she listened to Skinny Wilson stumbling over his reading lesson. And while he read:

"A soldier of the lee-gy-on lay adying in Al-gy-ers—"

"That is leegion, Tommy," corrected the gentle voice. And it is Aljeers, not Al-gy-ers. Read it again Tommy."

Tommy read it again rapidly before he should forget the accent:

"A soldier of the leegion lay adying in Aljeers—
There was lack of woman's kindness, there was dearth of woman's tears,"

But Sunny was praying in her heart:

"Oh, God, please don't let him have to go. Anyway not now before he is strong again. But if he *has* to go, please go with him. Guide him, bring him safely back again, and *please* help him to find Stormy—if he *has* to go."

Tommy was reading on:

"But a comrade stood beside him, as he took that comrade's hand,
Said he, 'I never more shall reach my own my native land.
Take a message and a token to some distant friend of mine,
For I was born—for I was born'"

He paused, but the teacher was praying frantically, "Oh Father, please bring him back to his native land. If he has to go don't let anything happen to him."

But Tommy's hand was raised.

"Miss Roselle, how do you say the name of that place? I can't pernounce it. There R-H-I-N-E. Is it Ro-hi-nie? Wasn't that guy one of our enemies? It sounds to me like the name of an enemy town."

Sunny suddenly roused to her job, and set the young student straight both on his geography and his pronunciation as well.

And over in a distant city another sweet girl named Cornelia was reading a letter from her brother "somewhere overseas." She paused and looked troubled over one paragraph and reread it:

Our whole company is worried over Stormy Applegate. You remember I told you he was with us several months ago. I guess you met him once at home before we left, didn't you? Well he was sent off on some very special mission among the enemy somewhere, a very dangerous errand. Perhaps to get information. But he's long time overdue now. The guess is that he's either a prisoner among those worse than fiends, or else he's dead. We don't know which, but they've about given up hope he'll ever be heard from. One thing is sure, no information has come from him and everyone is sure if he's alive he'd find some way to send us word. He's one who's never failed so far.

Then another girl bent her head and prayed for Stormy Applegate.

"Oh God, couldn't You find him?" she prayed. "You ought to know where he is. You could set him free if he's a prisoner, couldn't You?"

She wasn't a girl who was very used to praying, not for definite things like that. Not for lost soldiers whom she'd only met once and that casually. So, instead of the formal "Amen" that another might have added, she spoke the one word *"Please!"*

It was about then Stormy Applegate came in touch with a man from an "underground" outfit. Like a shadow he grew out of the darkness one night, and suddenly seemed to have been there a long time before Stormy was even aware there was a man.

Deadly weary, Stormy had been trying to forge ahead, hoping against hope that he could get around this occupied town, by the determined method of pushing on and trying to make it appear that he belonged in that region, hoping nobody would notice him. But suddenly he heard harsh footsteps ringing on the smooth road, loud voices, arguments, unmistakable accents of the enemy. Raucous laughter. Without doubt if he were seen he would be hauled to the authorities, and instantly his game would be over, the long hours of his weary journey traveled for naught, his mission lost. True, the information he carried was all in his memory. He carried nothing convicting on his person. Even if he languished in prison, or died, the enemy would never know what deadly knowledge he carried against them. But neither would his own outfit know the thing that would mean so much to the cause of righteousness if it could once be told them. Ah! He could not stay here. Less than a minute now and they would be upon him.

Quickly he turned, took a step to the left, across a ditch and dropped flat to the earth in the dark, holding his breath until the noisy enemy passed by, and lay wondering which way he might turn for safety. Having seen those arrogant men who dared to take another's country from them and march around assuming to rule it he knew now that it was useless for him to try to go alone through that town. He must somehow go around. And yet so confused, so weary he was, that he would fain have lain right where he was and called it the end. He could not drag himself up and try to keep going on.

It was then he felt the presence of that shadowy person who had been watching him for some time from a little distance.

He looked up and the shadowy figure seemed to draw nearer. It wasn't God. The man wore rough garments, like a laborer. Reaching out he touched the rough shoe and then drew back. It was after that the stranger drew close and dropped upon one knee beside him.

"Can I help you?" he asked in a low tone.

The tone was friendly. Did he dare to trust this shadowy stranger?

"I have come a long journey," he answered evasively. "I am very tired. I must rest a few minutes."

"Come, I will show you where you can rest safely."

He helped Stormy to his feet.

Stormy followed him, aside from the road. They came to a shanty built of boughs, behind a group of bushes, a pile of straw covered with tow bags was there. The stranger pointed.

"Lie down. No one will disturb you. And when you leave take the upper road." Again he pointed, and turning away, "God's blessing," he said, and vanished into the darkness.

Stormy hesitated, "And on you too, stranger," he said half under his breath.

He lay on that pallet of bag-covered straw, pondering. Had this been a real man, or one of the shadowy figments of his imagination? Rather, had it not been a vision that God sent to hearten him? He was too weary to think it through. Of course if this was someone sent from the camp to track him down, it might be only a trick to get him asleep and kill him for escaping from their clutches. It might well be that. The enemy seemed to enjoy such tricks. But if it was a trick he could not help it. He could not keep on much longer tonight, and if he tried to he would but fall somewhere else and be tracked down the sooner. He must get some sleep if it were only a few minutes. He would not sleep long. Besides, he was not alone. God was his guide and help. And there came to him a verse from his childhood: "My help cometh from the Lord, which made heaven and earth. He will not suffer thy foot to be moved: He that keepeth thee will not slumber."

He closed his eyes, and lifted his heart:

"Oh Lord, I'm in Your care. I'm trusting You to keep watch while I sleep. This is Your Stormy."

And in the morning when he woke, there beside him on the ground was food. Coarse bread and a tin of water, and on his eyelids lingered the memory of a frail hand touching him.

Of course that was the way God fed Elijah, but such miracles did not come today without a human instrument. Surely not an angel. Not that girl of his dreams for she was far away. His guess was that the shadowy man who had directed him to a resting place had done it and he thanked God. He ate his breakfast gratefully, puzzling meantime about the kindly stranger in the shadows last night. Was he one of God's men?

But he must not linger. The sun was over the rim of the world and light was growing brighter. He must get on. The upper road the man had said. "God, shall I take it? I'm trusting *You!*" he murmured in his soul.

He put the last morsel of bread in his pocket for another time of need and crept softly out from under the boughs. He wished he might thank whoever had brought him comfort, but he would thank God instead. The man would understand.

He looked about him, followed the path, an obscure one, that had been pointed out, and found himself mounting above the town, yet almost hidden from the world below. The way was not smooth, but he did not have to be so furtive about his going, and so could make progress. His limbs were stiff and still painful from the long journey of the days before, but he felt definitely rested, and much more cheerful. He no longer felt so alone. Surely some of God's messengers must be about somewhere. Surely sometime soon there would be someone whom he could dare to ask his location. And yet, he must not be impulsive. The enemy still had tricks to play. He must keep his eyes on his Guide.

He had been walking for what seemed hours when he suddenly rounded a tree, larger than most, and saw ahead of him down the leafy way, the figure of a man. Startled he watched him. The man walked steadily on ahead, and did not seem to see him. It made him uneasy, but he knew he must not show uneasiness. He must walk on as if he had a perfect right there. It would only lay him open to suspicion to seem uneasy. So he walked on. But when he rounded a little turn in the dim path he was treading, lo, the man ahead had disappeared! Now, what did that mean? Was it possible that he could hear quick footsteps farther ahead running? Oh, what did this mean? Was someone else hiding? And was there some way that he too could disappear before this person ahead could bring someone else to help seize him?

He looked around, but there was no sign of a way anywhere near him for him to hide. To the right, just beyond the bushes that made a wall at his side, he could see a bluff, with a sheer fall down into what looked like an old quarry, no trees nor foliage to hide behind. Just the rough open side of the blank mountainside.

He hastened his own steps, hoping perhaps to come within sight again of the stranger, but a swift survey at each turn of the way revealed only a lonely empty landscape, desolate, even in spite of the scraggly foliage that was a far healthier growth than any he had seen the day before. But as the day began to wane the way ahead seemed more and more desolate, filled with thick undergrowth that only seemed to him to be leading away from the direction he had hoped to take. Was this the intention, this detour that had apparently been mapped out for his unwary feet by that shadowy stranger who had seemed so kind?

He paused and sat down by the wayside to think it over before he would decide what to do, and to bow his head and consult his Guide.

Should he turn about and go back? Lose all that time? Or should he go on a little farther, and perhaps run into a nest of enemies who might take him captive again? Still, why should enemies take the trouble to lead him so far out of the way? They must know, if they knew anything about him at all, that he had come a long weary way, and must be weak and sick, almost starved. They would understand of course that he was in a state to be easily taken, without much force, or strategy. So why would enemies take all this trouble to mislead him?

And while he thought upon these things he took out the dry crust which he had saved, from the food the stranger had left for him that morning, and slowly ate it, trying to savor every crumb and make it taste to his sick imagination like a whole meal.

Suddenly he looked up and the shadowy stranger was before him again, looking down at him curiously, with almost a smile on his face.

"You found the way?" the stranger said.

"Yes," assented Stormy. "At least so far, I've you to thank for that. Or at least—I'm wondering?"

The stranger smiled vaguely, and looked at him keenly.

"You mean you do not know whether to trust me?" asked the man almost amusedly.

Stormy met his gaze across the dusk and smiled back.

"Well, something like that," he said, and smiled himself. "I was just questioning whether I was right. I am inclined to trust you. You certainly have been kind."

"Not very kind," said the man. "The bed on which you slept last night was not luxurious. The food left by your side was not very palatable. You see I wasn't sure if *you* were to be trusted," and the man smiled outright.

"Yes, well we don't know much about each other," said Stormy, "I was just asking God what to do."

The face of the other man softened.

"Yes?" said the man with a new tone in his voice.

"Well, I take my orders from Him too. Suppose we have a little talk. I'm not an enemy at least. Can you tell me anything about yourself? I don't want to pry into your secrets. What do you want? Where do you want to go? How could I help you, if I find that I *can* help you?"

Stormy grinned wearily.

"All right," he said, "I guess I owe you a little information. You've certainly been kind to me. The very fact that you can talk my language is an asset. Well, I'll tell you. I'm tired and I'm sick and I want to get home. If you can show me how to get there alive I'll be grateful."

"And home is America? Is that right?"

"That is right," said Stormy wearily. "How did you know?"

"Not because you are wearing an enemy coat," said the stranger pointedly. "You are from the internment camp."

"And you want to turn me back?" said Stormy wearily, his tired lips trembling. Then he gave a quick look at the other man, a man who was almost frail in his build, and yet there was about him a certain ruggedness. Still if he himself was up to his normal strength he could knock him out quickly enough and escape. But he was astonished to see a look of pity on that other face. Or was it just the shadows of the dusk that made it look that way?

"No, I have no desire to turn you back to that hell of existence," said the man in a kindly voice. "That is what we are here for, to bring help to any who are trying to get away. But it is not always easy, nor always possible. You will understand there must be great care, great caution. No impulsive moves."

"Of course not," said Stormy. "I think I have learned that."

"Perhaps," said the man, studying him carefully. "We shall see. But it may take some time. Arrangements have to be made. We are a long way from boats and air fields. But there are ways, at times. Then there have to be permits. Have you any identification papers?"

"Naturally not. They took those all away from me at that camp. Though I went with very little. It was a part of my job not to be recognized."

"I see," said the man. "Be careful not to tell that to everybody. We have a few with us who are not yet tried out. We cannot trust everybody."

"Of course not," said Stormy, "but see! I am trusting you."

The man smiled.

"And I you, or I should not have told you some of these things. I am warning you to be as cautious as if you knew we were all enemies. Something might be overheard even when you are talking with one you trust."

"I understand," said Stormy. "And I think I begin to see that you belong to some kind of an underground, loyal to your country, but in an enemy-occupied territory. France, perhaps? Am I right?"

"We do not put those things into words, my friend," said the man gravely, "we wait and see."

"I beg your pardon. I think I understand," said Stormy as gravely, "and if I transgress in any way I beg that you will let me know."

"I will, my friend. Now come. You need some food, and you need to sleep. It will be plain food and a humble bed, but you need have no fear. Come!"

Stormy followed him down a hidden path to an entrance. Inside there was a rough corridor cavelike in its structure, with several turnings, and at last a hollowed-out room furnished with a cot and blanket, a wooden table and a bench of rough boards.

"There!" said his guide. "Can you be comfortable here awhile?"

"Comfortable?" said Stormy. "It is like Heaven in comparison with the place from which I came."

"Yes, I know," said the older man. "I have heard others tell. Stay here now. They will bring you food, but I must go. I have other business to attend to. Stay here till I come back, or till I send you word. They will call me Pierre. Good night. God rest you!"

There was a quick handclasp, as between old friends, and the man was gone.

Almost at once a boy entered with a tray and food upon it. A bowl of steaming soup whose fragrance was most heartening, a plate of coarse bread, a pitcher of water and a tin cup.

The boy showed him where to wash, and then left him. Stormy sat down and ate every drop, and every crumb they had brought him. Then he washed and lay down on the cot drawing the blanket up around his shoulders. "God, I'm trusting You," he murmured, half aloud, as if God were standing there close beside him within that refuge. Then he closed his eyes and was immediately lost to the world in a deep profound sleep, such as he had not dared to take since he stole from that awful camp.

14

MILK and a kind of porridge in the morning for breakfast. Good milk, and good porridge! God be thanked!
Stormy was grateful. Later he lay down and slept again,
not even bothering to wonder how long he would be
kept prisoner in this semi-darkness. He was storing up
new strength, replenishing the life that had almost failed
him once or twice on the way here.

For three days Stormy rested a great deal, slept much,
ate all they brought him, found his way to the shower
bath and was refreshed. But when a fourth day came
without the return of his guide, Pierre, who had brought
him here, he grew exceedingly restless. Occasionally,
when he was sure there would be no one by to see him
he would put himself through some bodily exercises. He
did not wish to grow so soft he could not keep on with
his journey, in case all the promises Pierre had suggested
should fail him. He trusted the man, was sure he was
genuine, but by this time he had decided that probably
Pierre had promised more than he was able to fulfill, and
meantime he should get ready to break away and fend
for himself.

It seemed as he thought it over, that it might be an easy enough thing to do, to break away. The room he was occupying was, as he remembered his coming, but a few rods from the entrance door, and surely he could retrace the way by which he had come, after he was once out of this labyrinth of cavelike corridors. Yet he hesitated to make the break. Suppose Pierre should return and find him gone! It would be construed by him as breaking faith with him. It would show him that he had not fully trusted him.

And after all, even if he had to wait even twice as long as he had already waited, did he know any other method of hoping to get away from this dangerous location? It seemed sometimes that he was building hope upon a mighty frail foundation, but still he knew no other substitute for what had been promised.

So, on the fourth morning when they brought his breakfast, he asked the lad who fetched it if there wasn't some work that he could do, something to help in the scheme of the things out of which he was getting his living.

The lad looked at him speculatively, and said: "I'll ask." Later he returned and said: "Can you scrub and keep the washroom clean?"

Stormy agreed readily enough, and was promptly set to work, albeit he noticed that there were very few people around when he did it. Were they keeping him separated from all others until they should prove him out? Well, that was fair enough. So far he had not had access to much space beyond his own little room and the washroom. But somehow, though it gave him a queer feeling not to be trusted, he recognized the necessity and was content. But the scrubbing they gave him to do occupied but very little of the time that began to hang heavy on his hands, for he was getting slept out and really refreshed in body, and continually his rejuvenated mind grew more active. He tried to imagine what it would be like if he ever got back to his outfit. What he would say first and how the others would react to his coming. He began to count up the ones who had still been alive when he left, and found the fellow named Mayberry outstanding as a friend he prized. Oh, he hoped no mishap had befallen Mayberry. He was good in his line and was responsible for the destruction of a number of enemy planes. But sooner or later everyone, even of the best, fell, or was wounded or killed or taken prisoner, and even Mayberry might be among the list of casualties.

And then it came to him that not alone for his own sake would this man's loss be a catastrophe. There was that lovely girl, his sister Cornelia, the girl whose face had appeared to him in his own distress, with the appearance of an angel. If anything happened to her brother Cornelia would suffer. He did not want that. He found himself more than once praying that that would not be.

Then suddenly he told himself he was getting sentimental. He must snap out of this and turn his thoughts another way. There were others in his company whose friendship he prized. There was Barney Vance. He loved Barney. They were buddies. Even before he had brought Barney back from the battlefield in a dying condition, and hovered over him in the hospital while he was recovering from his own wounds, they had been like brothers.

Barney had still been in the hospital when he left on this expedition, still too gravely ill to be allowed to be sent home yet. Did Barney get well, or did he die? Where was he now? Boy! How he wished he might see him and talk with him for a little while! How they could talk about their Lord now, and he could tell his friend how again and again the Bible promises had been verified for him. How wonderful it would be if he had recovered enough to be able to go home. Supposing he had, and was even now back in their own land, if he should ever get back and be allowed a furlough he would go straight back to good old United States of America and hunt out Barney Vance. They would have a good old talk together. Yes, sir, that was a *plan*, and some day, if it pleased the Lord to let him go home, he would carry out that plan.

So he whiled away the hours, when there was nothing else to do, trying to keep his mind in a wholesome attitude toward the world in general, his world from which he had come.

And then one day, just as the long rays of the dying sun that reached a sharp brilliancy were slanting into the corridor beyond his doorway, where it shone every pleasant day for about ten minutes, he heard a sound. Soft footsteps along the stone floor, and then suddenly Pierre stood before him.

Stormy looked up with quick relief, an exclamation of welcome in his voice and eyes.

"You have come back!" he said with deep relief. "I was fearful that something had happened to you. I thought there must be danger to you whenever you went abroad."

"Yes, perhaps there is," smiled Pierre. "But then, isn't that the case with everyone, everywhere, even out in the world when there *is no* war?"

"I suppose it is," said Stormy. "And no one can die until God gets ready to call him. Yet humanly speaking we feel that we must care for our lives, unless duty demands otherwise."

"Yes," said Pierre with a smile. "Well, friend, this was duty demanding."

Stormy flashed him a look.

"I would not want to be the cause of anything happening to you, my good sir."

"Friend, those things are so tied up together that we have to trust our God while we are doing our best. That, I think, is what He wants us to do. And now come, I must tell you what I have accomplished. Come sit down beside me and I will show you."

Stormy sat down.

"These are your papers, and I have prepared this little wallet that you can strap beneath your garments where they will be safe. Now, listen, and set it all down clearly in your mind, for it should not be written lest it fall into enemy hands and do harm, either for yourself, or for our cause."

"I understand," said Stormy gravely.

"Tomorrow night you go out from here under escort. You will be taken to a certain point on the river where you will be met by a man in a boat, who is supposedly fishing. You will wait till the dark of the moon when he will draw up to the bank, and you will get into the boat and lie down. He will cover you with a dark piece of cloth, and will take you down the river to an airport where you will present this first set of papers, and you will be hired as an assistant radio operator. Did you ever do anything in the radio line?"

"Yes, I've fooled around with radio quite a good deal when I was a kid."

"Good! That will help! And then in due time you will be assigned to radio work on an airplane. When this plane reaches its second landing airport you will get off and take the train, and you will find all the data for that trip in this second little envelope. If anything happens that you fall into the hands of the enemy, you must quickly destroy all these papers, tickets and so on, and from that time you'll be on your own. But I have tried to forestall any trouble of that sort, except for some unforeseen occurrence. Try to hang on to your passport if possible of course. Now that was as far as I was able to arrange for you but that will carry you entirely out of enemy occupied territory, if all goes well. Can you make out from there, either to your fighting outfit, or to your homeland?"

"Oh, I'm sure I can. Yes," said Stormy. "But this is wonderful. I have God to thank for this as well as you, for I could never have worked all this out. Every step would have had to be an adventure, an experiment, and an exceedingly doubtful one."

"I hope that this will not be that now, not in any stage of the trip. But—will you let me know when you reach a place of safety?"

"I sure will," said Stormy, relapsing into his army dialect.

"You'll have to write in code," said Pierre, "else it might do us harm. We must not be found out for others' sakes. But I have written down an address to which you can write, which will be forwarded to me, and you must memorize it. Will you do that?"

"I will do that, my friend," promised Stormy solemnly. "And if in the days or the years to come there should be a time when I might do something for you to repay you for this great thing you have done for me, will you write to me? I will give you an address that will always reach me sooner or later."

"I will promise," said the man. And so with a "God keep you" they parted for the night, Pierre promising to see him the next day before he left.

Next evening when it had grown quite dark, and even the stars were hidden behind clouds, Stormy prepared to leave, and sat waiting for his escort.

Out across the world his friend Barney Vance fairly

haunted the office of the admiral, seeking permission to look for him, and his own regiment solemnly prayed in secret that he might be found. And over in America two girls, one golden-haired and one dark-haired with a face like an angel, were praying for him. So in a little while Stormy Applegate went out of the cavelike maze of corridors into the night, and an untraveled way, trusting in the strength of the Lord.

He went out, not having seen very far into that underground maze, not knowing its exact location, nor hardly any of its inhabitants, and unable to make known its deepest secrets even if he wanted to, which he did not of course. But he went out with a profound reverence and admiration for the beleaguered brave people who would not yield, and who were brave enough and strong enough to stand out against the enemy, against all odds.

He thought about that underground company a great deal during that first adventurous night, and it definitely registered in his mind as one more great reason why he ought to go back to his own outfit and help fight the rest of that war to the finish, just for those brave valiant men who were defending their rights and the rights of poor captive prisoners at the risk of their own lives. Always he could feel that Pierre was one of his most valued friends.

There might be perils on his way back, doubtless would be, but he felt that he was not trying to save his own hide, but seeking to convey vitally needed information to his officers that in the end would save lives and principles and promote peace in the future world.

So Stormy Applegate was once more on his way to unoccupied territory, and a great thankfulness grew within his heart. God had saved him once again, and he must go on feeling that every step of the way was directed by an unseen hand.

15

"WHO is the female snob at Kimberly's?" asked Hortense as she slammed into Amelia's hall and frowned at the girl who was usually so willing to lie down and let her walk over her. Therefore when Hortense was in an ill-humor she betook herself to Amelia's house and took it out on her.

"Oh," said Amelia with a sparkling face, "that's Mrs. Kimberly's niece from New York! She's come to visit her aunt. Isn't she lovely? I thought we might run in there and get acquainted and invite her to join our crowd."

"Not on your life!" said Hortense contemptuously. "She's not my type. Any girl who can afford to wear a mink coat like the one she had on her arm when she got off the bus this morning, and is so stingy or so unsophisticated that she doesn't buy lipstick is definitely not my type."

"Oh!" said Amelia with a sudden gloom over her pleasant morning smile. "But—Hortense, I read somewhere that it's going to be fashionable pretty soon to wear your face natural, and likely she knows it and has started doing it. They probably don't use lipstick in New York any more now, not among the very high class people."

"What do you mean, you little ignoramus? Where did you get all that stuff? On the radio I'll bet with some old maid crank talking that wants to make all pretty girls look as drab as she does. I can't abide people like that."

"Well," said Amelia thoughtfully, "she seemed awfully nice. I think maybe you'd like her if you'd meet her. Mrs. Kimberly introduced me this morning when I was passing the house, I wish you'd go over there with me to call."

"Not I!" said Hortense fiercely. "I want nothing to do with that type of person. And can't you see that we should be undoing all our plans if we got in a girl like that? She would make straight for Barney and absorb him. Literally *absorb* him, if you know what I mean, and then where would we be? As few young men as there are in town any more we can't afford to do that."

"Oh, well, I suppose you're right," said Amelia ruefully. "I said practically that to Jan Harper yesterday when she suggested asking that Roselle girl."

"What do you mean? That little school-ma'am? The perfect idea! As if *we* would mix with her. Besides she's years younger, isn't she? Just a mere baby. Jan must be crazy!"

"Well, she says she had Barney over singing at church Sunday night. You know she's playing the organ over at the Old First now. And they say he can sing. Really *sing!*"

"Do you mean he sang a solo?"

"Yes, Jan said so. She said everybody was crazy about it."

"Well, he used to have a good voice when he was a kid, but if they get him roped in with that church crowd it will spoil all our plans. They're awfully straight-laced, almost as bad as Barney's mother used to be. They don't approve of anything that's any fun. They call it 'worldly'! Can you imagine it? We've got to get to work as quick as Barney gets back and put a stop to that church business. Did you call up Roxy this morning? When did she say he was coming back?"

"She didn't know. She said he had to see somebody in the service about when he might have to go back overseas, or something."

"Oh, for Pete's sake! Are they going to send him back again so soon?"

"She didn't know. She said he wanted to go hunt for a buddie of his that was missing."

"What folly. Barney *would* do a thing like that. That's the way his mother brought him up. We've got to get to work in a hurry. Although I don't believe the army would allow him to go off on a fool errand like that. If a fellow is missing it means he's *missing,* that's all, and they better give him up and concentrate on somebody else. Just suppose everybody who has somebody over there they admire should take it into their heads to run over after their friends. Why there wouldn't be any room left for war! *Imagine* it! But no, we certainly don't want that little school-teacher-child, nor that other important looking Kimberly girl either. Forget it, Amelia, and let's call up our guests and postpone our parties till Barney comes, and then we've got to get going without delay. Now I'm going around to that Roxy person and get it out of her where Barney is, and how long before he is coming back. This is all bunk that she doesn't know. I'll *make* her tell." Hortense gave her henchwoman a contemptuous look and marched out of the house.

On her way down the street she passed the Kimberly house and there was Cornelia Mayberry out in the yard picking white violets. Hortense studied the cut of her handsome frock and resolved to get one like it if she could. She hurried on her way, not even glancing again toward the beautiful girl who looked up as she passed.

Hortense found Roxy out gathering eggs from her chickens, giving her a bad half hour, but getting not one atom of information from her. Roxy was canny, and Roxy certainly did not like Hortense.

"It's a pity you didn't have several children to look after," was Roxy's parting shot as Hortense swung indignantly off toward the gate. "If you had some children you wouldn't have half so much time to run around after young men." But Hortense strode on pretending not to hear, and Roxy, enjoying the scene, especially as she saw two women approaching down the road within earshot grinned mischievously.

"Hortense!" she called clearly, as if she had forgotten to tell her something, and Hortense paused and looked around haughtily.

"Do you know what you ought to do? You ought to go around to the Community Center and look after some of those refugee children they've undertaken to care for. That would be a real heart-warming task and give you good practice for the time when you have some children of your own. I'll speak to the committee about you if you'd like the job."

"Oh, shut up!" said Hortense in her most disagreeable tone, and swung around to open the gate and march on.

"Still," continued Roxy to herself, grinning amusedly, "I'd be sorry for the children if *you* had charge of 'em."

Hortense as she pranced on her way was thinking bitter frustrated thoughts. An old playmate, a returned soldier, highly spoken of for his bravery, had returned for a furlough and *she* was being kept entirely in the background. Her frantic efforts for his notice had been futile.

She hadn't been able to get him to do anything she planned for him, and that little light-haired school teacher had carried him off to church in triumph. Made him sing for her. For of course *she* had been the one who had done it. "Sunny" he used to call her, just a *child!* And *she* was presuming upon that old acquaintance when she was a mere baby! Bah. She had to get even with that girl. Teach her where to get off. Show her that she wasn't even in the picture with *her* and her group of friends. A public reception in the town hall would be a good idea. She would start that going right away. Barney could be made to sing at that too, some army song. And a speech about his experiences could be demanded by the whole crowd. That would be popular enough. Everybody liked Barney, and those that didn't know him had loved his mother anyway. It wouldn't be hard to get up such a thing. And really the town ought to recognize what he had done in the war of course. She had heard some of the women of the women's club suggest it, but why shouldn't *she* get ahead of them and start it herself, thereby getting all the glory?

She walked on well pleased with herself, and decided that she would begin by putting that Margaret Roselle in her place.

To that end she mounted the steps of the schoolhouse when she came to it, clattered down the bare hall on her high spindly heels, opened first one door and then another, slamming them resoundingly behind her when she found them empty, until she came to the big sunny room where Margaret Roselle was hearing the history class recite.

Without knocking she flung the door wide open and stepped into the room, and all the pupils turned and looked at her wonderingly.

The teacher looked up in surprise.

"Oh, did you want something?" she asked in her gentle voice.

"Yes, I did," said Hortense. "I came to find *you*. I'm giving a dinner at my house Saturday night of this week. I expect to have several service men and some girls, and I wanted to know if I could hire you to wait on the table. You'll be well paid, of course."

Sunny looked at Hortense, astonished, and then she laughed.

"Oh, I'm sorry," she said, "I'm afraid you've been misinformed about me. I don't do that sort of thing."

"Oh, *really?* I thought you would do *any*thing to earn a little money," she said disagreeably. "But surely you would do it for the cause of patriotism. There are to be some service men there."

Sunny gave her a distant smile and answered firmly: "That would be quite impossible."

Then turning back to her class she said: "Now, Mabel, you may recite. What was the great question that came up before Congress at that time?"

And to Hortense's amazement the young teacher went calmly on with her work, ignoring the outsider in the room, and all the children astonishingly did the same. Were they trained to such utter concentration on their work, or were they simply indignant at the insult given a teacher who was evidently a great favorite of theirs? Hortense was not so dense that she could not sense this feeling of the children through her own chagrin. She had even failed in mortifying the girl she disliked so much. Disliked without any reason too, except that she was younger and prettier than herself.

The end of the matter was that Hortense finally went home and retired behind locked doors to have one of her terrific sick headaches.

Amelia, calling up later to ask some trifling question,

and being told that Hortense had a headache and was gone to bed, got herself together and went over to call on the interesting Miss Mayberry, taking care that this visit should not come to the ears of her erstwhile mentor. But she did not invite Cornelia Mayberry to join their group. She wouldn't have dared, not after what Hortense said. But she did admire Miss Mayberry, and somehow she felt that Hortense was getting a trifle too much what the more conservative people called "ultra." Somehow Amelia's natural bent was toward things more quietly conventional.

Amelia went home very thoughtful, and even much more intrigued by Cornelia Mayberry.

High on the fifth floor of the office building where he spent a great deal of his time, the admiral sat in his comfortable desk chair across from Barney Vance whom he had just welcomed warmly.

Out the open window they could look off down the silver winding of the river, and see a busy steamer puffing on its way. Down below there somewhere was the beautiful whiteness of the lovely Lincoln Memorial, and across from it the ethereal beauty of the famed cherry-blossom walk not so far away but that they seemed somehow related, as if like lovely funeral blossoms they marked the passing of a great, white, powerful soul.

Barney had waited some time for this interview, and now that he was within the presence of this his father's old friend, he almost shrank from making known his request. For suddenly it had become to him something presumptuous that he should ask permission to go on a special search for the one for whom doubtless the army had already made all the search that was necessary. And yet it was Stormy, *his* Stormy who had saved his life, and therefore Stormy could in no wise be so important to anyone else as to himself. Even though Stormy had rendered notable service to his country.

But now the time had come and he must speak.

"I'm here in behalf of a buddy of mine who saved my life and brought me on his own wounded shoulder, back to my outfit. If he hadn't done it I would have died six months ago. The doctors all said so. And while I was still in the hospital he got well and was sent on another special important assignment to get facts about the enemy that were needed. Well, he didn't come back before I left, and I have reason to think he hasn't come back yet. Meantime, I'm invalided home somewhat indefinitely, under doctor's order. But Admiral, I want to go back *now* and search for my friend. Or at least to find out somehow whether he is alive, and I can save him. Admiral, I wonder if you could tell me whether what I want to do is at all permissible, or possible, while I am still in the army; and if it is, whether you can help me to pull the right ropes to get permission? I'm still in the army, you know."

The admiral sat staring at Barney with his heavy white eyebrows lifted, and his eyes keen and earnest, studying the young soldier before him. He sat with his elbows on the arms of his mahogany chair and his long white fingers just touching their tips. And then he began to ask questions.

"I suppose you know that this is a very unusual and irregular thing you are asking?" he said gravely.

"Yes, I was afraid so," said Barney, "but somehow I had to come. I knew you could advise me. You were the only one I knew to turn to, and I feel this very much on my heart. I must know whether my buddy is alive, and needs help. I must give it if I can."

At last the admiral spoke:

"Well, my dear fellow, that is very commendable, of course. I do appreciate your feeling for your friend, and especially as he helped to save your life, but I'm not just sure whether what you want *can* be done or not. It is quite out of the ordinary, of course. I should think, as you are still of the army, it is your duty of course to ask about the ruling in such a case. I understand you did some very commendable work yourself. You seem to be wearing a good many ribbons and medals of honor, and your present proposition is quite within the character you seem to have established while in the service. But now, I will not say what can be done. I will of course be glad to help you in any way allowable I can, but I should say that the very first thing would be to ascertain, if possible, just how much is absolutely known of your friend, and whether he is still missing. There are ways of course to get that fact established beyond a doubt, and it is well to do so before the question of your going after him is gone into, also to find out your own status with regard to health. I will make it my business of course to find that out. If you can be around here for the next twenty-four hours I *may* be able to tell you just what the prospects are, and by that time I shall have looked into the ruling about what you want to do, and *perhaps* can then let you know what is possible. But there is one question I would like to ask just for my own curiosity. Just why did you think *you* would be able to find your friend when the whole army has failed in doing so? Have you any inside information that you could not pass on to another? It seems a pity for you to have to use up your leave time and strength going on a long journey like that, that could be more economically accomplished by one nearer to the place where he disappeared. Had you a special reason beyond your own obligation for what he did for you?"

Barney looked troubled.

"Yes," he said earnestly. "You see I have been to the same place myself where we thought he was being sent, and we talked together a little about what one could do if he got stuck there. I thought—perhaps it's only a hunch,—but I know the region pretty well, and I think I'd know where he would hide out, if he didn't get caught in an internment camp they've got up there."

"I see. But suppose he is in the camp? You couldn't do anything."

"I figured that a man outside could help better than the man that was inside," said Barney, "and I know what Stormy would do under such circumstances."

"Yes, that might be," said the older man, "but you must bear in mind that you would probably be shot by the guards while you were trying to save your friend."

"I'd rather be shot to save a life like Stormy's, than to be shot just in a battle," said Barney fiercely. "Excuse me, but you don't know Stormy yet," said Barney. "Some day maybe I'll bring him here to see you, and then you'll understand."

The older man smiled:

"You're very sure he's alive, aren't you?"

"I am," said Barney.

"Very well then, we'll get to work. Suppose you write down all the names in the case, and the location, your company, your engagements, and the address where I can contact you when I get information."

Barney handed out a folded paper.

"It's all written here," he said, "everything you need to know. Now, I'll thank you for giving me your attention and time, and get out of your way. And I'll be praying."

"What?" said the admiral. "What did you say?"

Barney smiled half shyly.

"I said I'd be *praying.*"

"Oh," said the admiral, studying the young man, "in other words, since you didn't get quite what you hoped from me, you intend to take this to a higher court. Is that it?"

Barney's smile was very reverent and engaging.

"I took it to a higher court before I came here, sir!"

"Oh, I see!" said the surprised admiral. "Then it's rather up to me to find out what the higher court would have me do," he said thoughtfully, as if an entirely new idea had been presented to him. "Well, I'll have to look into that."

Then Barney, saluting, went out, and the admiral walked to his window and stood staring toward the ribbon of silver river shining in the distance, and the dome of marble that honored a great man who was not afraid.

Presently he turned and touching a button on his desk that called his secretary, directed her to start an investigation to find out what was definitely known of the whereabouts of one William Applegate, more familiarly known as "Stormy."

Then he went to his desk and wrote two or three brief notes to personal friends in the service, called up a few more on the telephone, and all in the matter of what could be done to find Stormy Applegate. But Barney Vance had wandered out under the great pink and white row of cherry trees to look up and talk to God, as he had promised the admiral he would do.

16

BARNEY came back to Farmdale at the end of the week, having sent two post cards back to explain his absence. One to Sunny, promising to return in time to help her with the choir Sunday; the other to Roxy ordering buckwheat cakes for breakfast Sunday morning. Both cards bore beautiful pictures of the famed cherry blossoms. But not a word of all this leaked out to the gang that was chasing in vain after Barney Vance.

But it was only Sunny who carried in her heart an ache because she was fearful that Barney might be going back overseas before he was physically able, and so she prayed the more.

About the middle of that week Mrs. Kimberly sent for Margaret Roselle to come to supper and get acquainted with her niece Cornelia Mayberry. And Margaret came, pleased that Mrs. Kimberly had selected her to meet her niece instead of the other crowd, although Mrs. Kimberly was a friend of Margaret's mother, and *would* do that. But the fact that she was asked perhaps prejudiced her in favor of the niece beforehand.

The two girls studied each other politely while the

introductions were going on, and then smiled and sat down to talk.

"It is your brother who was in Barney Vance's company overseas, wasn't it?" asked Margaret. "Barney told me about him, how fine he was."

"Yes," said Cornelia cordially, "and Jim wrote me that I must be sure to see Barney, and he sent a lot of messages to him. There was a message about Stormy Applegate. He said I was to tell Barney that they had heard nothing further from Stormy. The outfit is sure now that he was taken prisoner, and there seems no hope they will ever see him again. He knew Barney was anxious about him when he left for home."

"Yes," said Margaret anxiously, "I've heard about Stormy. But Barney doesn't believe he was killed. He says that he went in the strength of the Lord, and he believes he will come back."

The other girl gave her a quick appreciative look that was almost embarrassed. Cornelia Mayberry was not used to speaking of things religious in ordinary conversation. She hardly knew how to answer, and yet she realized that this other girl was something fine and unusual. She wondered if her brother knew of her. He had never mentioned a girl named Margaret, nor even a girl named Sunny, which was what her aunt Mrs. Kimberly called her. She would have a lot of things to ask Jim when next she wrote him. Meanwhile, she was here to stay a few days at least, surely until Barney came back and she could deliver her messages from Jim. If she liked it here, and this girl proved as pleasant as she seemed to be at first sight, she might stay longer, instead of joining her cousins at the resort where they usually spent the summer together.

Cornelia's young cousin Sam Kimberly had come into the house now and was in the next room turning on the radio, hastily, as if he were hunting for some special station. The girls were talking and not noticing the radio, till suddenly Barney's voice spoke out clearly and came into the living room as if he had just walked in at the door.

"Friends, I'm glad to greet you, and to say hello to all in my native land."

Margaret looked up and caught her breath, exclaiming:

"Why! There's Barney now! Listen! That's *Barney* talking!"

Her eyes were bright with joy, and her cheeks a lovely shy pink. Cornelia looked up interested and began to listen, and also to watch this other girl whom she was just beginning to know.

But almost at once Cornelia Mayberry knew she was listening to a very unusual voice, and did not wonder that her brother had written so enthusiastically of Barney.

"Friends, I don't like to talk about myself, nor what happened to me over there in the war, but they have asked me to tell you about the most thrilling experience I had while I was serving, and though I shrink from talking about it, yet I guess you have a right to know. For it was your war I was fighting, and I was glad to be able to do what I could to attain the victory for which we are all waiting so anxiously."

"Oh!" said Cornelia. "This is what I wanted to hear!"

But Margaret said nothing, only listened with her heart in her eyes, and her breath bated, as if she feared to lose a single syllable.

Barney's clear ringing voice went on, describing vividly in a few words the day and the command that sent him out on that most thrilling experience of his life, till the listeners almost felt they heard the bursting bombs, the heavy firing, and seemed to see the thick smoke that filled the air, the strain and excitement of the moment when the enemy was met. Oh, they had heard other returned soldiers tell on the radio about such experiences, but this was different, hearing somebody they knew, or knew of intimately, talk! And Barney's way of telling was different from any other they had heard.

Out across the road in Amelia's home somebody yelled over from the Harper house. "Amelia is Hortense there? Tell her to turn on Washington. Tell her Barney Vance is speaking on the radio!"

The girls in the Kimberly house did not hear that outcry, but Amelia did, and there was immediate action. Then the radio spoke out, and the girls who had assembled at Amelia's house to arrange for that public reception they were planning to put on for Barney as soon as he came home, stopped talking to listen. But all plans ceased while Barney's voice held the audience breathless.

"It was that last plane shot that got me," went on Barney. "I was just thanking God that the attack was over and I could go back again to my outfit and feel that I had done my duty and both myself and my plane were without injury, when I got the warning. There was another plane coming, and coming fast. I had only time to cry to God for help. I somehow knew this was going to be worse than all the others. But I worked fast and did my best till just at the end when I felt that sharp burning pain strike my shoulder and run down my arm, and I knew I was helpless so far as further fighting was concerned."

Margaret sat there gripping her small hands together, her lips pressed, her eyes like great dark pools of horror, Cornelia, watching her, said to herself "How very much she cares! And no wonder! A man like that!"

But Barney's voice went on:

"Somehow I got my plane down, for the other plane had gone on after it had done its deadly worst, and just there, there was no more enemy in sight. Afterwards I was weak with the pain and loss of blood, and probably unconscious for a long time. But later, when the sun went down I came back to myself. I knew when I saw my plane that I could not fly back. I knew there was an injury to my pipe line, and that I must start at once and try to get back under my own power. So I just cried out to God, and told Him how I was fixed, and asked Him to help me back. I crept out and crawled along the ground till I got to a woods, and knew I was on the right way, but every foot I went was agony, and I did not know how long I could hold out. I found a brook, and drank, but it was hard for me to reach. That helped a little and I got to my feet and went on a little way, but I was faint and dizzy from loss of blood and soon I ran against a tree in the dark and fell, striking my head on a stone perhaps. I must have been unconscious for a long time, but finally I came to again and tried to creep on, but I couldn't make it. I went out like a light and lay there, with my last conscious thought that this was the end. Then, what seemed a long time after that I felt a hand touch my face gently. I felt a light strike my eyelids, a flashlight perhaps, and then I felt myself lifted to a shoulder, and carried on over the rough ground, slowly, along the trees, stumbling but still going on. And I found out afterward that the man who was carrying me was my old buddy, Stormy Applegate, and that he was badly wounded himself when he picked me up. But yet he carried me back to my outfit, all the way back. And friends, I'm glad to tell you of that great thing my friend did for me. I wouldn't have been living today if he hadn't brought me in in spite of his own injury and pain.

"I was a long time getting well. At first they thought

I never would. But my buddy, Stormy, got well before I did, and they sent him out again on a special assignment involving great risk, and calling for much skill and cleverness. He said good-by to me, knowing we might never again meet on earth, and he has never yet come back! They think he was either killed or taken prisoner by the enemy, and they say there is nothing more that they can do. But I believe that he is still alive, because he told me he was going in the strength of the Lord. I would ask no greater privilege than if I might go myself out there in the enemy land to find him. But since I have not obtained permission yet to do that, friends, I'm asking *you* if you will pray for Stormy Applegate, for I believe he is still alive! I thank you for listening to me."

A storm of applause followed the silence that fell as Barney ceased to speak. And over at Amelia's house Hortense's voice came out sharp and clear:

"For the love of Mike! Can you beat that! He certainly has got it bad! We'll have to get him over that religious complex quick or he won't be any good at all in *our* world. Imagine all that sob stuff about another soldier! That's his mother coming out in him."

But over at the Kimberly's the two girls had tears on their cheeks, and the young brother appeared in the doorway with an excited face. "Wasn't that great, cousin Cornie?" he said, his voice all husky with feeling. "Imagine him wanting to go back! But that's Barney for you. He was always that way."

"I should say it was great!" said Cornelia. "Was he always that way, Margaret, or is it the war that has made him so?"

"No, he was always a good deal that way. He was a Christian you know. He had a wonderful Christian mother. But still, I think the war has done a good deal, too. And you ought to hear him sing! He sang a solo in church last Sunday night. I think he'll sing again next Sunday. He has a beautiful voice, but it's the way he gets the words across that is so great. It's just like a sermon preached when he gets done."

"I should like to hear him," said Cornelia gravely. "I think I'll stay and hear him. That will be something to tell Jim about."

Margaret looked at the beautiful girl before her, and a sudden qualm of jealousy shot through her. It had been hard to see Barney taken over by the set that went with Hortense, hard worldly girls, that was different. They weren't his kind. But here was a girl that was worthy of him, a girl so beautiful that she could not hope to compete.

It was only an instant that such a thought flashed through her mind, and then Margaret, being what she was, put it instantly from her. Why, she could love this girl herself, and why shouldn't Barney like to meet her, and to take her for a very special friend? And who was *she* to feel badly about it? If this was what God was planning for Barney why she must be glad for him. She must not think of herself. Both she and Barney were God's children, pledged to His service. And after all Barney did not belong to her. He was just an old friend, and would be, of course, all her days, no matter what else came to him. So quickly she smiled cordially.

"Yes, do stay and hear him. I know you'll think he is fine," she said. "He really has a very unusual voice, and it will be nice to tell your brother about it of course."

"I could see he had an unusual voice just from his speaking," said Cornelia. "I will stay. My aunt was hoping I would stay longer, and since I know you, and like you so much, perhaps I will."

"Oh, that will be wonderful!" said Margaret smiling.

Then suddenly Cornelia spoke again:

"Say, tell me about Stormy. Have you met him? Do you know him?"

"No," said Margaret, "only by hearing Barney tell about him."

"Then you wouldn't know much about his life, would you? I was wondering . . . is he . . . a religious man?"

"Oh yes," said Margaret positively. "He is a Christian. Barney told me about his experience. I think he was just a church member before he went to war. But afterward he became quite changed. When he first went across the sea and came into the region of actual war, where he saw death in all its ugly realities, and the terrible possibilities of going out to do his duty, he said he met God. It was one night when he was flying through the sky, going into his first engagement, and he realized that he might be going straight into death. But he felt he didn't know God well enough to stand in His presence with his life just as it had been on the *old* earth, living for *himself*. It was then that he felt God came to him. Of course he had heard the way of salvation preached all his life, but had never really accepted it, nor even fully understood how great God's love had been to let Christ take his sins upon Himself and die for his soul. And he said that night in the clouds as he went forth to meet the enemy, God met him in the way, and talked it all out with him, *made* him understand it, in just those few minutes. It didn't take long, because one needed only to get that one glimpse of the Lord Jesus to understand it all. Just to *know* Him. And Barney says that Stormy always tells people that if you've never known Jesus you can't understand, or you can't be ready to face death without Him. After that all fear is gone, and it makes all the difference in the world. That is why he is so eager and anxious to make other people know his Lord."

"That sounds very wonderful," said Cornelia. "I didn't know he was like that. You see I met Stormy once myself. It was before my brother went across. They were in the same training camp. I went to camp to see my brother before he was being sent away, and Stormy was there. Only they didn't call him Stormy then. It was Bill Applegate, and they hadn't known each other very long. I don't suppose they had talked about such things then. They were almost new acquaintances, but they liked each other from the start, and he was one of the first fellows Jim wanted me to meet. He said he liked him a lot. I liked him too. He's a very interesting fellow, and awfully good-looking, a strong fine face. One you can't forget, even if you've never seen it much. I've never forgotten him. You haven't ever seen him you say?"

"No," said Margaret, "only a snapshot Barney carries around with him. He says he owes his life to him, you know. But Stormy *is* very handsome I think, with a great wide lovely smile. Of course *I've* been praying for him too, ever since Barney told me about him. But didn't your brother tell you about his being a Christian?"

"Not exactly," said the girl with a puzzled look. "Only one thing he said. When he wrote us about Stormy's being lost he said, 'Some of us fellows can't believe that Stormy is gone. We think he'll turn up, yet, because when he went away he waved his hand and said good-by, and he said he knew he'd be all right, because he was "going in the strength of the Lord"'. You see my brother and I were not brought up to talk freely about religious things. It wasn't done in our family, and Jim would think he was saying a great deal to tell me even that. But I've wondered. You think that Stormy is definitely a Christian now, do you? And that when he went away on this mission that phrase he used that he was 'going in the strength of the Lord' was something real, not just an empty phrase he used, like good-by or good luck or something of that sort?"

"Oh, no," said Margaret with a smile, "I *know* it was real. You see just before he left he came to the hospital where Barney was and they prayed together. That is Stormy prayed, mostly, for Barney was still very weak. And Barney says it was a wonderful prayer, full of utter trust. Barney seems very sure he is still alive."

"Well, I don't know as I have any right to pray, for I'm not a very good Christian, but I've been praying too, ever since Jim's letter came telling about his being missing in action, I've been praying every night. I can't somehow seem to forget him. I've waked up sometimes at night and prayed for him, and yet I don't know him really well, you know. Oh, you'll think I'm a sap, I suppose, but somehow I wanted to find out if you knew."

"No, of course you're not a sap," laughed Margaret. "I'm glad you are a praying girl. That makes me feel as if you and I could be real friends. We love the same Lord, and speak the same language."

Cornelia looked a bit hesitant.

"I don't know if you would think I'd qualify for that honor if you knew me better. I'm not so sure about loving the Lord. I don't really know Him well enough to be sure I love Him. And I'm quite sure I can't speak many sentences in your language, for I've never learned. Perhaps you can teach me."

"*Teach* you? Oh, I'll be glad to *tell* you what I've learned, but you know it is the Holy Spirit that must really do the teaching."

"I'm afraid I don't know much about the Holy Spirit," said Cornelia, filled with awe. "You know I've never read the Bible much. I tried once or twice, but I just couldn't understand it, and got discouraged and gave it up."

"Oh, I'll take you to our Bible class," said Margaret. "It's wonderful. And we're all so interested the people never want to leave and go home. It meets one evening a week, and we have one of the best teachers in the city, so clear and interesting. I know you will enjoy it."

"It sounds good," said the formal city girl, a bit bewildered to find there was so much to this matter of being a Christian.

So the two girls sat and talked. Finally, Margaret took out the little Testament she always carried in her hand-bag and began to explain the lesson on John that they had had last week, and both were so absorbed in it that they were surprised when Mrs. Kimberly called them to dinner.

Mrs. Kimberly, listening to their pleasant talk at the table, and watching their animated faces, felt that she had done well in selecting this girl to companion with her niece.

But over across the street the plans were going forward for that reception that Hortense was getting up for Barney. And Mrs. Kimberly would have been surprised indeed if she could have heard them plotting just as if the young war hero was the special property of Hortense, and would do exactly as she told him to do.

17

BARNEY Vance came back from Washington late Saturday afternoon, after having received word from his friend the admiral that he had found that he could do nothing in the matter of Barney's request until the authorities had cabled overseas and received a report from his company, both concerning Stormy, and about Barney's state of health when he was sent home. And it might be some time before that matter was cleared up and it was definitely established that Stormy was still counted missing.

Much disheartened Barney came back and went at once to Margaret Roselle's home. Somehow it seemed the natural thing for him to talk it over with his old friend.

Margaret's face glowed with pleasure when she saw him turning in to the lane, and her eyes were shining happily as she ran down the lane to meet him halfway. But she had no idea how that little act of welcoming him back thrilled Barney.

He hurried up the lane, watching her as she came, so graceful, lithe and lovely. She seemed like something of his own, and yet he told himself he must not think that. He did not know but that she was promised already to someone else. Yet that thought appalled him, for he found that he had really been thinking of her all the time he had been away, counting on telling her about his experiences, counting on coming back to her. He had seen many good-looking girls while he was in Washington, for the admiral had introduced him to a number of them who were near his mansion, and they were all interesting girls, yet none so sweet nor beautiful as this dear girl. How was it that she had grown up so unspoiled, as lovely of heart as she was of face?

His heart quickened as her feet hurried toward him and he saw the welcome in her eyes. She was glad to see him. He had a sudden wish that he might take her in his arms and hold her close, but he put it from him. He was not a young man who had been used to going around making love to girls. His mother's teaching had gone deep on that subject, and he had an utmost reverence for womanhood. But he did not remember to have felt like this before about any other girl. Was it this brief absence that had made this girl Margaret seem so much more desirable than she had, even when he first saw her that morning among the apple blossoms?

But these were foolish thoughts. She would think him crazy if she knew. It must be just that he was tired and excited, and had been through a heavy strain in Washington, with all the noise and bustle, and the anxiety about getting his wishes across to the right authorities, who *might* permit him to go after Stormy. Yet oh, it was good to get back to this girl and her sweet sympathy! And she was as much interested to pray for Stormy as he was. He had felt lonely while away.

And now she stood before him, her hands out in eager welcome, and he reached out and took both her hands in a close clasp, and felt the thrill of a great joy sweep over him, the sweetest thing he had ever experienced. Why he wanted to fold her in his arms and hold her close! What was the matter with him? Was he falling in love? No, of course not, and he must not frighten her. She would think he was crazy! Besides, it was broad daylight, and there were three men in the neighboring field, and her mother might be looking out the window.

"I'm—so—glad to get back!" he murmured, shame-facedly, but kept on holding both her hands.

"And I'm so glad you've come!" said Margaret shyly. "It has seemed you have been gone a long time. And I am so anxious to know what you did." She added quickly, "Do you have to go away soon again?" and she almost held her breath waiting for the answer.

He smiled down into her face. He was still holding her hands in his warm clasp. He pressed them closer, and her own nestled in his happily.

"Not yet," he said half ruefully. "It seems anything like this takes a long long time. One would have time to die before rescue came. But it looks at present as though there wasn't much chance of my getting to help Stormy, not yet anyway."

She drew a breath as if of relief.

"I'm glad," she said softly, "I was so afraid for you. Yet I do think God will send him back. I have been praying so very hard."

He was watching the changing eagerness on her sweet face, the look of joy in her beautiful eyes, and suddenly forgetful of the watching eyes about that farm, he murmured softly:

"You *dear!*" And then without warning, and certainly without a definite intention beforehand, he stooped quickly and kissed her! A fervent earnest kiss. And her warm lips responded, lingering with a thrill of joy upon his own, and brought that desire to fold her in his arms again. Only now there was the consciousness of that wide world of three men, and a mother, perhaps in observation. He was astonished at what he had done almost impulsively, for his whole life training had been along the lines of careful deliberation before acting. But this time his heart had taken the lead, and he was glad.

Suddenly Margaret drew back a little, looked up at him with a question in her eyes, then dropped her face against his shoulder.

"Oh—Barney—" she breathed fearsomely, and there were quick tears upon her lashes.

It was then that Barney forgot any possible audience and drew her close within his arms, bringing his face down to hers again.

"Forgive me dearest," he murmured to her little pink ear that he found beneath his lips. "I ought not to have done this out here in plain sight. I ought to have waited. But oh, *darling!* Sunny! *I love you!* I love you, and I couldn't wait! I felt as if I had got home and you were mine. Maybe I am presuming. Maybe you belong to someone else." He held her off and looked deeply into her eyes, but she laughed back at him with a joyous happy lilt.

"No," she said with a sweet little tremble in her voice. "No, I don't belong to anyone else. I've—*always*—belonged—to you!"

And then he had to fold her close again.

"Oh, my darling!" he said.

The sharp ringing of a scythe against a whetstone brought them both back to consciousness, and they looked around. Suddenly, from a tall tree near by a wood thrush thrilled out a silver note of exultancy, and their two hands clasped again joyfully.

But the men in the field were very busy trying to get

done a swath before the set of sun, and the mother in her kitchen was just putting a pan of puffy rolls in the oven for supper. Nobody saw the little love scene but Margaret's twelve-year-old cousin, come over to pick berries for supper; and he, canny before his time, looked on with eager pleasure.

"For Pete's sake! Now ain't that something?" he murmured to himself. "I didn't think they'd have that much sense to pick each other out. But I'm mighty glad before that Hortense got her finger in the pie. I *like* Barney a lot. He's *swell!*"

Needless to say there was no reception for Barney Vance *that* night, because the plotters had not been able to find out just when Barney was to be at home. And they didn't find out that he was home until the next day, for Margaret and Barney took a walk in the woods after supper, and came back to the house under the soft moonlight, Barney's arm about her, her hand in his, with no workmen, nor twelve-year-old cousin around to watch. They were going back to the house to tell Mother Roselle what had happened to them.

And there was no fear in their going, for they were quite sure of the welcome that awaited them. Mother Roselle was very fond of Barney, and had been one of his mother's dearest friends.

Hand in hand they made their way slowly, and now and again Barney would draw her closer to his side and bend to kiss her softly.

"Oh, Sunny, my darling Sunny! To think you are mine!" he whispered in a glad voice.

"Oh, but I haven't told you everything that's happened since you went away!" said Margaret suddenly remembering, as they went up the path to the house. "A new girl has come!"

"Oh, what a nuisance!" said Barney. "There's only *one* girl for me, and I have her right here beside me."

A sweet solemnity of joy swept over the young girl's face. She needn't fear to present the other girl, since she had such dear words of Barney's to hide in her heart.

"But she's very lovely," said Margaret.

"Not so lovely as my girl," insisted Barney.

"Oh, but she *is,*" said Margaret eagerly. "She's much *much* better looking than I am."

"Oh, no, she isn't. She couldn't be," said Barney. "I have never seen a girl as lovely as you are. That's true. I've never looked at girls at all. They didn't attract me. Not till I saw you."

"But wait until you see her," said Margaret laughing. "She really is lovely."

"Must I see her?" said Barney, putting on a martyrlike look.

"Oh, yes, you must *see* her. That's what she's here for. To see you. Her brother was in your outfit overseas, and he wrote and told her to see you. She is Mrs. Kimberly's niece."

"Oh," said Barney suddenly remembering, and looking bored, "I remember now! I was to go and call on her. Mrs. Kimberly called up Roxy and asked her to send me. She's Jim Mayberry's sister. But seeing you put her completely out of my mind. You've met her? What's she like?"

"Yes, I've met her and I think she's lovely! We're friends already. Mrs. Kimberly invited me over to see her. And Barney, she knows your Stormy. That is she met him once at camp. And she and I have been praying for him. She has some messages from her brother for you, and one is that Stormy has not been heard from yet, and most of the men think he is dead, for they say if he were alive he would never have let them go so long without some kind of a message. She says her brother said, 'Because he went in the strength of the Lord,' she thinks that means that maybe her brother is saved too."

"He *is*," said Barney with conviction. "We had a talk before I left. But he's not much used to talking about such things. He's a nice kid, a bit younger than Stormy and myself. Well, then, dearest, we'll go and see her together, shall we? But not tonight. I want you all to myself tonight."

"Of course," said Margaret, nestling close to him as they reached the door and must now go in.

And then the door was opened by Mrs. Roselle, and she gave one quick glance at their faces, their clasped hands, and a great joy came into her own face to welcome them.

"Oh mother," Margaret said, "you don't know what has happened to me!"

The mother turned a searching glance to the smiling soldier's face, and Barney rose to the occasion:

"I *love* her, mother, do you mind?"

"Mind?" said Mrs. Roselle, beaming at them. "Do I *mind*, did you say? Why yes, I mind very much, dear boy. I couldn't ask anything better for my child than to be loved by you," and she put up her arms and gave Barney a warm motherly hug and kiss.

"And I know your own mother would be very glad about this too, dear son," she said, standing back and looking at them happily.

"Yes," said Barney fervently, "I know she would. I know she *is*, for somehow I can't help feeling she knows all about it, and has perhaps been watching us."

"Of course," said Margaret's mother. "And now come in at once. The chicken and waffles are all ready to be served, and I know you must be hungry, even if you have found you love each other. Come."

So they went in to a happy supper. And Sam the young cousin came to supper too, and sat and stared and grinned at the two. He could hardly eat his own share of the waffles and chicken, so awed he was by the thing that had happened within his sight. For every time he remembered what he had seen down the lane, he grinned to himself about it, till his face was a study in growing up.

After supper they all went into the kitchen and washed the dishes, and Barney dried them. Then the two young people went to the piano and sang a little while, selecting the music for the next day's services.

So Barney stood by the piano while Margaret played, and exulted in the fact that he was now privileged to put his hands possessively on the dear girl's shoulders, and know that she was his.

Outside down the highway went Hortense's shiny car, with a gang of loud-voiced revelers, bound for a roadhouse wherewith to pass the time, till they could get hold of Barney and complete their plans for a public reception.

And back at Mrs. Kimberly's Cornelia sat and talked with her aunt for awhile, listened to the war news on the radio, and then took some books from the library and went up to her room to read. Somehow this Saturday night was the lonesomest day yet, for Margaret hadn't been over all day, and she didn't even know whether Barney had come back yet. She almost wondered why she was staying in Farmdale. Yet when she got up to her room the book she actually picked up to read was the Bible that her aunt had loaned her. For she thought she would make another try at reading it and see if there was anything in it she could understand now in the light of some things this new girlfriend had said.

She tried several places to read, but somehow they

didn't seem to mean anything to her, till at last she opened by chance to the book of John, and then remembered that Margaret had said that was a good book to begin with. So she read on, becoming more and more interested as she went deeper into the story, for she saw it was a story, and an interesting one. And when at last she laid down the book and prepared to go to her rest, she turned out her light and knelt down by her bed and prayed. Yes, she had been praying every night of late for the lost soldier called Stormy, but this time she ended her prayer with a petition for herself:

"Oh Lord, I think I need to be born again, like that man Nicodemus I've been reading about. Won't You please show me how, and make me able to pray acceptably for Stormy Applegate? Because I want him to come home. I want to see him again, and understand what You can have made of a strong splendid man like that."

Then she got into her bed and closed her eyes, but somehow she kept seeing the strong handsome face of the young soldier who had been with her brother in the camp the day when she was there. And she kept imagining him a prisoner, hungry, suffering, unable to help himself, and yet cheerful, and full of faith in God in spite of it all.

Of course her idea of Stormy was partly the product of hearsay, things her brother and Barney and Margaret had said of him, with a little background of her own memory of Stormy's handsome sparkling face as he had talked to her at camp. But her thoughts had hovered over the memory of him so much that he seemed very real to her. What would she have said could she have known that it was her face that had come to Stormy Applegate in his weariness and fever and utter discouragement, and that he had thought she was God's angel sent to help him?

Where was Stormy now, tonight? Now while she had been praying for him? Could it be possible that he was still alive? Why was she so certain he was? Was it just because his believing friends thought he was, or because God had put the thought in her heart? And why should she care so much? He was practically a stranger to her.

At last she feel asleep, dreaming her way across the clouds to see a plane in the distance, with dangers and fogs and enemies to hinder, and only a hidden passport and some trifling papers to see him across the border of a land that was enemy-infested. Would Stormy ever come back? And would their faith be justified?

While Cornelia slept the Holy Spirit was working a change in her heart, a conviction that she needed to be saved, to be born again. That she must accept what Christ had done for her to make good in the scheme of His plan of salvation. Though she had had so little teaching and so little understanding of the Scripture that she wouldn't have understood what part the Holy Spirit had in calling her to accept Christ as her own Saviour, nor have comprehended what this change meant that was coming upon her, making her so dissatisfied with the self she had been, the self she had hitherto felt was rather to be admired. Popular, that was what she had always been in the circle in which she moved. But now, was she popular with God? Could she claim any request from Him and hope to have it granted? Not perhaps if she had not accepted His offer of salvation, the kind of salvation that Margaret Roselle believed in. The kind that Stormy, and his friend Barney believed in. Yes, and her own brother Jim. Life wasn't just a round of pleasant things as she had always believed, with her stage set with luxury. There was war, and death, and separation; and a God with a place in Heaven to which one might go through accepting the gift of salvation. And there was a devil, and a hell, and a death that was not just the body dying, but the soul being separated forever from God and good and all righteousness! It was all very terrible, and she must find out how to understand it.

These things had begun to dawn upon Cornelia's soul since she started to pray for Stormy Applegate.

18

CORNELIA went to church the next morning with her aunt, and watched the choir file in, the sweet young organist at the organ, playing exquisitely. There was something about Margaret Roselle that intrigued her greatly.

Then she took to studying the faces of the choir, especially the tall young man who came in last and took a seat at the end next the organ, rather out of sight. Could that be Barney? He wasn't quite so good-looking as she remembered Stormy to have been. Or was he? He *was* good-looking. And he was in uniform. Of course that must be Barney. If he sang a solo she would know. Or would she? There might be other young soldiers who sang solos, and Barney might still be in Washington of course. But this one certainly *was* good-looking who-ever he was. Though probably the uniform made all of them look rather well. She knew her own brother was quite impressive in his uniform.

As the service progressed she was impressed by the reverence and dignity and quiet interest of all. She noticed, too, the quick look that passed between Margaret and this soldier by her side. It was an intimate smile, as of people who had known one another long, and were very fond of each other.

Then came the solo, and Cornelia was sure it was Barney. Somehow he was so like the man her brother had described. And there was something about his face that seemed so in keeping with his wish to go back into the region of war to find his friend and bring him back.

It was a most unusual song, not a regular solo. Just a hymn, but it was sung almost as if it were spoken, and yet the voice was very beautiful, mellow, tender.

I see a Man at God's right hand,
Upon the throne of God,
And there in sevenfold light I see
The sevenfold sprinkled blood.
I look upon that glorious Man,
On that blood-sprinkled throne;
I know that He sits there for me,
That glory is my own.

The heart of God flows forth in love,
A deep eternal stream;
Through that beloved Son it flows
To me as unto Him.
And looking on his face, I know—
Weak, worthless, though I be—
How deep, how measureless, how sweet,
That love of God to me.

He sang as if it were so real to him, as if that love of God he was singing about was the most precious thing to his soul. And that blood that was sprinkled was the most priceless coin that could be paid for a sinful soul. Cornelia found herself with tears slipping down her cheeks, and she was aghast at herself. She hurriedly flicked her wisp of a handkerchief over her cheeks, and Hortense and her crowd sitting staring in the back seat, studied her and saw the tears. What was the idea, that high-hat crying in church? Had she recently lost her lover, or some close relative? There didn't seem to be anything in that solo to make anybody cry. It didn't make good sense anyway. What was it all about and why didn't Barney use his head selecting a song, and get something really peppy, something that would show off his voice if he had such a fine voice? But what was that poor sap crying about, anyway? Then they turned and gave attention to the singing again, and they decided that Barney hadn't picked the song at all. That girl Margaret must have picked it and she was a regular sob sister. But what on earth did it mean anyway and who was a man on God's throne whose glory Barney was claiming for his own? Well, he probably didn't understand it himself. Then they turned their attention to the beautiful girl who was sitting with Mrs. Kimberly and listening with her heart in her eyes. Did she know Barney? Was he one of her long lost lovers, or what?

But there was one girl in that audience who had got something out of that song, one girl who listened afterward to the dear old preacher, telling in such simple terms what the story of the blood meant, and who was the Man of the song, the Man Christ, sitting on God's throne, presenting His blood to pay for our sin. Bringing it right down to souls, so that they couldn't help understanding what it all meant.

But the hymn at the close of the sermon was more in the language Hortense's crowd could understand. Barney sang the verses and the choir softly came in on the chorus.

On Calv'ry's brow my Saviour died,
'Twas there my Lord was crucified,
'Twas on the cross He bled for me
And purchased there my pardon free.

And then the choir came softly in on the chorus:

Oh, Calvary! Dark Calvary,
Where Jesus shed His blood for me . . .

"For Pete's sake," whispered Hortense quite audibly, "why don't they sing something cheerful? I should think a returned soldier would want to talk about something besides death and blood, or do you suppose they've got so used to it all that they don't know the difference? That's the reason I never go to church. They are always so gloomy, harping about sin and dying. As far as I'm concerned I want to have a good time while I do live, and then when I die that'll likely be the end of me, so what?"

But Amelia who sat next to her was listening to the last words of the song and made no response, so Hortense turned her attention to the very smart hat that Cornelia was wearing. She might be from New York and be very snooty, but she certainly could pick out the clothes, and Hortense prided herself that she knew good clothes when she saw them.

When the service was over those girls in the back seat pranced promptly up to the choir platform and greeted Barney as if he had been away for a year. They congratulated him on his *wonderful* singing, and his *marvelous* voice. And they simply raved over him so that the rest of the people in the church hung back and looked askance. Then Barney began to see what was going on, and smilingly sought to dismiss his would-be intimates.

"Well, that's awfully good of you, friends," said Barney smiling, "but suppose we cut out this flattery. I see somebody down there that I must speak to, and you'll excuse me I know," and he courteously slipped past Hortense and stepped down from the choir platform.

But Hortense was not to be sidetracked so summarily. She had come to church for one purpose only and she did not intend to go home without accomplishing it.

"But Barney, there's something I must tell you," she shouted at him. "You are in for a surprise and we felt that you should know about it beforehand, so there won't be any mistakes."

"A surprise," said Barney turning with almost a frown. "Tell me quickly, please. I am really in a hurry." For Barney could see that Mrs. Kimberly and her young guest were starting down the aisle toward the door.

"Why, yes of course, but when you hear what it is you'll see I can't be hurried about it. It is quite important. We have planned . . ."

Barney saw by her tone that she was going to absorb a good deal of time with her important surprise.

"Well, then if you can't tell it quickly, perhaps you'll excuse me please, for a few minutes. There is someone I must see before they leave," and he slid out past Hortense and hurried down the aisle toward the Kimberly pew.

"Oh! *Indeed!*" said Hortense in that cold offended tone she could assume so disagreeably on occasion.

But Barney was not listening to her tone, and there was nothing for Hortense to do but stand and frown at him, as she watched him go down and speak to Mrs. Kimberly and be introduced to "that obnoxious snob" as she had come to call Cornelia.

She saw the cordial greeting between Barney and Cornelia, and watched the interested smiles that each face held. She saw that there must be some special bond of interest between those two, and little by little she edged her crowd down the aisle till she was fairly standing in on their converation.

She heard Barney say:

"Why, I don't know. I'll ask Margaret just what she has planned for tomorrow," and then he looked toward the organ.

Margaret had but just stopped playing and was picking up her music and getting ready to leave, and Barney called, across the heads of those girls who had tracked him down:

"Margaret! Margaret! Can you come down here a minute? Mrs. Kimberly wants to ask you something."

Margaret gave her beautiful smile and hurried down toward them, but Hortense leaned forward and spoke:

"But Barney, we've simply *got* to speak to you a minute at once. It's *quite* important. I am sure these people will excuse you. We've arranged for tomorrow night to give you a reception in the Woman's Club House, and there are some arrangements about publicity that simply won't wait another hour, or we shall be too late to carry out our plans."

Barney lifted his head toward Hortense with raised eyebrows and a sudden sharp note of dissent in his voice.

"What was that you said, Hortense? A reception? To *me?* Not on your life you don't! No, lady. You'll simply have to change your plans, for I won't appear at any reception, and that's flat! I'm here for just a little while, and I don't want to be held up for admiration. I haven't done anything more than all the boys did who went out there to fight. I've just done my duty, and you folks over here don't need to waste your time plastering admiration on me. I just want to meet my friends in the ordinary everyday walk of life. And I want you folks to go on fighting on the home front the way you were when I got home. There isn't time for parties and frills."

His voice was almost genial as he finished, though it was still very firm, and he did not look at Hortense as he grinned to them all in general, but turned smilingly back to Mrs. Kimberly.

"But Barney," protested Hortense, "you can't *possibly* mean that! All our plans are made and we've hired the hall and got the invitations out. You *can't* do that to us!"

"Sorry, girls, but I'm afraid I can. I'll just have to return the compliment and say *you can't do that to me!* I'm just Barney Vance and not a little tin god, so please don't get any more of these things going. If you've got your plans made so you can't stop them, turn your show into a war bond sale. That'll please me better than anything else."

"And will you *speak* to us?" called out one of the girls, realizing that Hortense was not getting on so well.

"And *sing?*" asked Amelia.

"Why?" asked Barney smiling.

"Don't you think you owe this to your own towns-people?" spoke up Hortense bitterly.

"*Owe* this to you? How? Haven't I been out fighting for you? Why do I have to get up and show off before you? Of course, I'll be glad to say a few words of greeting, and tell everybody to buy all the war bonds they can, if that will do you any good! That is I'll do that if I'm not in Washington. I'm liable to be sent for any minute so I can't really *promise* anything. When did you say this was? Tomorrow night? Okay. Come if I can. Now Margaret, shall we walk over with Mrs. Kimberly?"

"But you'll sing for us too, won't you?" pleaded Amelia.

He gave her a quick look. Poor Amelia! She didn't

often have the nerve to plead, or hardly *speak* when Hortense was there.

"Why, yes, I'll sing if you'll let me sing what I want to."

"Oh, but we want some of the popular songs you sing overseas! We don't want your long-faced hymns," wailed out Hortense.

"Sorry," said Barney, "I'll have to do the picking. I can't sing everything you know," and he gave her a mischievous grin.

"Come on Margaret, let's go," he said, and slipping his hand in her arm he led the way after Mrs. Kimberly. The gang hung back disconsolate, with Hortense mad as a hatter.

Margaret and Cornelia were smiling amusedly.

"I suppose they planned it to please you, didn't they Barney?" said Mrs. Kimberly in a kindly tone.

"Well, perhaps. We'll give them the benefit of a doubt," said Barney, "but if you ask *me* I'd say they planned it to please *themselves,*" and he gave his twinkling grin. It made them laugh outright.

So they walked home with the Kimberlys and went in for a few minutes while Cornelia and Barney talked of her brother Jim, and of Stormy Applegate who had not come back yet. Then Barney and Margaret walked back to her house. Hortense, meantime, behind the window curtian, watched them enviously. There went Barney, just as he always had done, going with somebody else, when she had tried with all her might to get him for herself. Why was it that she failed? Well, at least he would come to the reception for a little while, and he would speak about war bonds. That wouldn't give him any room to drag in religion. And she'd see that he sang some of the popular music too, even if she had to ask somebody else to call for something. But all the rest of that Sunday she was bitter and disagreeable to everybody around her, and at last Amelia in despair said:

"Oh, for Pete's sake, Hortie, why do you have to be so jealous? You can't be *it* all the time, you know."

"What do you mean, *jealous?* Do you suppose I'd stoop to be jealous of that little colorless mouse of a Sunny? She, going around posing as 'Margaret' now, as if she were some great personage. She was always called Sunny! And what's Barney being so sweet to her for? Just because she plays the organ in the church? What's the church, anyway, nobody that's very important goes to *that* church. As far as I'm concerned I don't intend ever to enter the door of that church again, after the way I was treated this morning. The *idea!* When I told him we had got up this reception to *honor* him!"

"Oh, you're too sensitive, Hortie," said Janet Harper. "Barney was only half joking all the time. But I don't believe, really, that he honestly likes parties and speeches and things. Boys never do, don't you know that?"

"No, I don't!" responded Hortense snappily. "The general run of men *like* to be flattered, and be called 'it,' and praised, and all that. If you ask my opinion of *men,* they're all a conceited lot, and the only way you can get anything out of them is either to praise them or else *feed* them."

"Oh, Hortie, that's not so! I don't believe men are like that!" said Janet Harper again.

"Well, *really.* I don't suppose it matters what *you* believe! You never had any brothers, and you don't have much to do with any other men, so you wouldn't be supposed to know."

Janet sat back subdued and kept out of the conversation for a whole hour, while Hortense raved on about the church, and the way they had been treated that morning.

Nevertheless, as evening drew on, they all planned to go to church that night, to hear Barney sing again.

Hortense did her best to get Amelia to write Barney a note, asking him to sing that lovely little gem of a song called "My Prayer."

"That'll keep him off those dismal religious things he delights in," she said, "and he certainly can't object to that. It sounds real ethical to me. It's about doing good to others, or something on that order, 'making some heart glad' I believe is one line isn't it? I remember I sang it for a Christian Endeavor prayer meeting one night when I was quite a little girl."

But while those girls knew that song pretty well by heart, none of them ventured to quote the words, and Amelia refused point blank to make any request of Barney for *any* song.

But they all went to church.

The song that Barney sang that evening was "Ye Must Be Born Again."

This time it was Cornelia who sat as one hypnotized as she listened to the words, so clearly telling over the story she had read in the Bible the night before, and she wondered if she would have any opportunity while she was here to ask Barney about being born again and how she could get it for herself.

The sermon that night was very stirring, given by a young chaplain from the near-by camp, who was a man after God's own heart, and knew his Bible better than most. Even Hortense's hardened, contemptuous, empty little heart must have been searched by it, as she sat for a time staring fiercely at the young preacher, her eyes wide and almost frightened. Then, in the midst of it, she turned utterly away and putting her elbow on the back of the seat and her head down on her hand, yawned openly, and closed her eyes, pretending to be asleep. Margaret, watching her from the little mirror over the organ decided that she was greatly stirred by that simple earnest sermon; but if she was, she certainly did not intend that anybody should know it.

But when the service was over, Barney, after talking with the young minister for a few minutes, suddenly disappeared, nobody knew where, and Margaret after her organ stopped, slipped out the back door and somehow nobody could find either of them after that. "Queer, wasn't it?" said the girls who had been hanging around hoping to have another talk with Barney.

"Well, I'm not surprised," said Amelia to a group of them. "I wouldn't think he'd stick around after the way you treated him this morning, Hortense."

"Treated him?" said Hortense. "How did we treat him? I don't know what you mean. I certainly don't think he's being very courteous tonight, do you?" But nobody answered her.

Barney and Margaret had gone out the back driveway of the church and were sprinting rapidly in the direction of Margaret's home.

"I wonder what he sees in that little washed-out school-teacher!" said Hortense angrily as she lingered for a moment at Amelia's door to say good night and suggest what to do about collecting the sandwiches that had been promised for the reception Monday night.

"Well," said Amelia thoughtfully, trying to speak the truth and yet avoid angering Hortense any further, "I suppose it all depends on one's point of view. I don't think most men admire much make-up, do you?"

"Meaning that you think *I* wear too much?" snapped Hortense.

"I didn't say that," said Amelia. "I suppose it all depends on the type you admire."

"Well, good night. I think I've taken plenty for one evening. I'll go home and gather up a little strength to try and get through tomorrow night. And after this I'm *done* with homecoming soldiers, no matter how popular they are. I wonder what this Stormy fellow is like? I'd like to see him. He sounds interesting to me. I'll bet that religious complex is all a figment of Barney's imagination. Makes a nice sob-stuff story. Ten to one he's having the time of his life somewhere among so-called enemies, while Barney goes around posing as his would-be rescuer."

"Why, Hortense! I thought you *liked* Barney."

"Well, I thought I did too, but I've taken as much off him as I'll take from now on."

19

ON the way home Barney and Margaret discussed the reception of the next evening.

"It's a doggone nuisance," said Barney disgustedly. "I just knew those fool girls would do something unpleasant. Of course I can't refuse to go, because of the rest of my old friends, but I just hate to go through a thing like that. We can come away early, though, can't we? It wouldn't be necessary for us to stay till the last cat is hung, would it? I wouldn't want anybody's feelings to be hurt, of course. *My* mother's old friends! And after all it is nice of people to want to say hello to me. But couldn't we say we had another engagement, and get away?"

"We!" said Margaret with a troubled look, "why I don't think they would expect *me* to come. I never went with their crowd."

"Say, look here! You don't mean to say this isn't a community affair, do you? Isn't *every*body invited?"

"Well, I'm sure I don't know," laughed Margaret. "Nobody's told *me* anything about it."

"Well, you *better* be told! If you don't go *I'm* not going, that's definite!"

"Well, of course I *could* go I suppose. I could get mother to go with me. But really, I don't believe they expect *every*body. Not the older people. Or maybe they do, but I haven't seen any notices, and it wasn't in the paper. Besides, how could they tell people? They didn't know whether you would be here."

"Well, we'll go over, you and your mother and I, and if we find there is only that crowd of highfliers there, we'll only stay about ten minutes, and then we'll have another important engagement. I'll fix that up. I certainly am not going to waste a whole evening on that crowd. Besides, you and I have a lot of time to catch up on, and we can't afford to waste it."

Margaret slid her hand into his, they walked happily along together and soon forgot the reception, and everything else but their love for each other, and their joy in being together.

"Oh, Barney," said Margaret. "You don't know how wonderful this all is for me. To have you singing in our dear old church, to have you here again, even if there is the dreadful possibility that you may have to go away again. It will be something to remember I have had. To know it is me you love, and I'm not left outside, the way I have so often been. No, I ought not to have said that, for I really never cared that I was left out by those other girls. I never could have enjoyed being with *them*. They do not love the things that I love. They delight to snub me, and jeer at anything they understand I like. But there! I should not talk that way. Some of those girls could be very nice, if only they wouldn't listen to Hortense so much. But say, Barney, did you watch her face during the sermon? I do believe she was listening."

"I thought she'd gone to sleep the one time I saw her."

"No, I think that was only a pose. I saw her in the little

organ mirror. Before she leaned her head on her arm and closed her eyes they were wide open and she positively looked frightened! She always tries to pose as being one who isn't afraid of anything, but somehow I had the feeling that that sermon got under her skin. I think she saw for a minute or two what it would mean to get sent away from the presence of God forever. I don't think it ever occurred to her before that hell was like that. An absence of all righteousness, all that was good, separation from God forever. I think it really frightened her. And when you sang that last song about the blood she looked frightened again. I don't believe that after all one could hear a sermon like that and not mind the thought of spending all eternity in the company of devils in hell. I suppose maybe nobody has ever tried to make her understand, before."

"Yes," said Barney thoughtfully. "I suppose she has a soul that needs saving. Somehow I never realized that with regard to her. She has always been so self-sufficient, so sure of herself. Still, of course Christ died for her, as well as for all other unsaved souls, and probably we ought to pray for such people the more. Make our lives a better witness before them, rather than to be sarcastic and try to shy away from them. But they don't want our prayers and witnessing I'm afraid."

"No, I suppose they don't," said Margaret earnestly. "But I guess we can't go up to God's throne and expect to meet Him with unburdened souls, if we haven't at least told them about our so great salvation."

"That's right, dear. And I guess I'm glad I said I'd go to their reception. It wouldn't have been Christian to be selfish about it. But we'll go, and we'll do our best to witness, even if Hortense did try to stipulate we shouldn't have any long-faced hymns. Well, perhaps there is some way of getting a bit of truth across in a bright and cheerful way that will make them want to find our Lord. That's the business of Christians of course, to be witnessing everywhere, even when we can't just really like the people. They certainly need the truth even more than attractive ones."

"Oh Barney dear!" said Margaret softly. "How wonderful that you turned out to be like this! And how happy your mother must be to know about it! I'm sure she knows."

"Yes, so am I," said the young soldier, folding his girl's hand close in his clasp. "But there's something else that is wonderful to me, and that is the fact that God kept you so sweet and dear and fine, brought you up in His love and strength, taught you to serve Him; and then let you love me. That seems to me the crowning joy, that you love me, and that some day if God lets me live, you can be my wife. I don't think there is anything else that is so sweet on this earth as for God to have given me the love of a girl like you."

"Oh, Barney! That's such a wonderful thing for you to say. And just a few days ago I was almost afraid to have you meet Cornelia Mayberry because I was afraid you would fall in love with her. Just think of my being jealous and selfish like that!"

"Dear!" said Barney, laying his other hand on hers that rested on his arm. "You dear! That you should care like that! But, my darling why should you think I would ever turn from you to that other girl? She's a sweet attractive girl, I own, and I think she'd make a very nice friend for—well, somebody else—but I could never choose her instead of you, my little Sunny girl! She's a lovely girl, and she's asking a lot of interesting questions about the Lord, and the Bible, but you needn't ever think that anybody can possibly be to me what *you* are, and I hope will always be, my precious!"

So they walked slowly along the moonlit road, and talked of things of Heaven and things of earth, and rejoiced more and more in their love for each other. It was characteristic of Barney that he did not think of that reception that was to be tendered him but once and that was to be glad that his best uniform was cleaned and pressed and in order. He would have nothing to do to get ready for the affair except to put it on. He went to sleep pondering what he could say in the few words he had promised, that would not only sell war bonds, but would also be helpful to some soul in the dark of a war-torn world. Not too much. Just to go on record and show what he stood for.

As Margaret was busy with her teaching the next morning Barney had arranged to call on Cornelia and answer some of her questions about the Bible over which she seemed deeply troubled. But his going did not escape the young gang who were undertaking to establish an espionage over him.

"There! Look out there! There goes Barney into the Kimberly house," announced Janet Harper who had just arrived at Amelia's with a basket of sandwiches she had been collecting for the evening festivity. "You see you were wrong, Hortense! He's caught on to the new girl now. I guess he's not so keen on Sunny after all."

"Oh, that's nothing!" sniffed Hortense, who was there to borrow more teaspoons and cups. "He's got to go somewhere, hasn't he, just to pass the time? And Sunny is a schoolteacher, so he can't go around with her week days. Evenings maybe, but not daytimes."

"Did you invite Sunny and her mother?" asked Amelia's mother.

"No I didn't," said Hortense. "I thought it wasn't any

business of theirs, and anyway it's been announced now. There's a notice on the post office bulletin board. I simply don't care for that silly Sunny, and I resent Barney's trotting her around everywhere, so why should I invite them? And I didn't ask the Kimberlys either. If anybody else wants to they can, but I'm not going to."

"Well, I think that was very rude," said Amelia's mother. "They are lovely people, and dear friends of Barney's."

"Not any dearer than we are," sneered Hortense, "and not half so interesting. They are awfully dull to have around I think, and always trying to run everything their way, if you ask me. We don't hit it off well together at all," and Hortense got up and went to the front door. She had known she would meet with opposition if this subject came up but she wasn't afraid of Mrs. Haskell anyway. She was just like Amelia, hadn't the backbone even to make a fuss. So the subject died down and was forgotten.

Mrs. Kimberly invited Barney to stay to lunch, but he excused himself, saying he had telephone calls to make and letters to write, and must go home. The truth was he wanted a little time to himself to rest and think over the coming affair that evening, and he had promised Margaret to meet her at the schoolhouse and take a long walk, and he did not intend to allow anything to break up that plan.

So Cornelia and Barney sat down with the Bible and went over a few verses that Cornelia had been puzzling over, and then she began to ask questions about Stormy. She listened intently as Barney told of Stormy's religious experience, meeting God out on his way to die as he supposed, and how he had been serving Him ever since.

When Barney went back at noon Cornelia sat with the Bible in her lap and her eyes far away. Then she took out a little snapshot of Stormy that her brother had sent her, and she had treasured ever since. She studied the tiny picture, trying to read into that handsome laughing face all the beautiful experience about which Barney had been telling her. And that afternoon, out on their long lovely walk Barney said to Margaret:

"Do you know, dear, I wouldn't be surprised if your friend Cornelia is more than half in love with our Stormy. She says she's only seen him that one time that she visited the camp. But of course he is very stunning looking, and has a great way with him. But she seemed to want to know more than anything else if Stormy was really saved, and did I think one could always be sure that a dead Christian *always* went to be with the Lord when he died. I wonder if she thinks Stormy is dead?"

"Well, I'm afraid she does, Barney. You see everybody has been telling her that he must have been killed or he would have sent some word. That he never let his regiment go uninformed if there was any possible way to let them get a message. Her brother wrote her that just yesterday."

"And yet she is praying for him to come back."

"Yes, but she thinks it is only wishful thinking that makes us say we are sure he is alive. And perhaps she wants to be sure that she can meet him in Heaven, since it seems so unlikely she will ever see him again on earth."

"Poor child!" said Barney. "And poor Stormy! What a girl she would be for him! He deserves somebody like that who would love him a great deal. But he would never presume to ask her to marry him I'm afraid. He knows she belongs to a rich family, and while he hasn't an inferiority complex, he would feel it was presuming when he has no fortune to offer her."

"Oh, but that would be foolish! She is not at all like that. She doesn't think of money."

"Well, no, I don't believe she does, but *he* might."

"He'd better not meet her then," said Margaret with a troubled look. "That would be an awful thing, to love a man and not have him ask her to marry him just because she has a little money even though he loves her. How utterly silly. A nice girl couldn't ask him, and will she have to go alone all her life because he has such an idea?"

"Well, I don't know if Stormy would feel that way. Perhaps he's got more sense now. I think he has come so close to bigger things than any on this earth that he might not think of such things any more. He *might* only ask her if she was saved. And now I think of it, and remember how he talked when I last saw him, I believe if he loved her, that would be the only thing that might hinder him from asking her to be his wife. He would ask first, 'Does she love my Lord? Is she saved?'"

"Oh," said Margaret earnestly, "I'm so glad he is like that! I do wish he might come back. It would be so great to have those two come together. I believe Cornelia's brother wishes it too, from some things she read to me from her brother's letter yesterday. Was he a Christian too when you knew him?"

"Well, kind of a shy one I guess. I never was just sure where he stood. But it must be talking with Stormy has made a difference in him. Or else meeting death out on the battlefield so familiarly. She read that letter to me too this morning, and I wondered. He wasn't like that with me, the last time I talked with him. But then I had been very low myself, and they wouldn't let us talk long."

Margaret reached over and slipped her hand in Barney's, pressing her fingers close.

"Dear," she said softly, looking up into his face, "I'm so continually thankful to God for saving your life and bringing you back to me. I keep thinking how dreadful it would have been if you had never come back and I had never known you loved me."

The look that passed between them then was one to be remembered.

They came back when the sun was going down, and the long sweet spring twilight was beginning, hurrying at the last, because they remembered that they must really be dressed up tonight.

"Oh, I forgot to tell you. I asked Mrs. Kimberly and Cornelia to go with us tonight," said Barney. "I knew your mother wouldn't mind, and I found they hadn't had an invitation. So as I am the one who is being recepted I thought I had the right. You don't mind do you, dear?"

"Mind! Why of course not. I was going to suggest it myself, only I forgot. We can stop for them as we go down. Mother will be delighted. She loves Mrs. Kimberly. And you must remember neither mother nor I were invited, either. There will be strength in numbers. And especially as we are in the company of the guest of honor."

"Why, yes, of course," laughed Barney. "It would be a pity if I didn't have any rights at my own party. Come, I think we had better hurry."

"For the love of Mike! Will you look at what's coming!" exclaimed Hortense to Amelia, as the guest of honor entered with the four ladies. "He would do something like that, wouldn't he? Bring a lot of snobs and chaperons. But my word! Look at their clothes! Even that little mouse of a Sunny has a new frock I never saw her wear before. It isn't half bad, is it? One of those new shades of blue I've read about. You don't suppose she borrowed it from the New York girl, do you?"

"Of course not," said Amelia sharply. "That Mayberry girl is a foot taller and several inches wider in her shoulders than Sunny. And why should Sunny have to borrow clothes? She's making plenty teaching school, isn't she? Besides, I heard Mr. Werner say the other day in the bank that Mrs. Roselle is wealthy herself. She gives a lot to the church they say."

"How foolish!" said Hortense. "I wonder what she gets out of doing a thing like that."

Then she roused herself to gather her reception committee together, stand in line, herself at the head, and introduce the incoming guests, though most of them had known one another all their lives.

But the pleasant friendship of the evening didn't depend upon Hortense, although she had hoped it would seem that way. The people were all glad to be there, for they loved Barney, and they had also loved his precious mother. So they just took over the evening themselves and didn't bother in the least about Hortense and her gang. So Hortense found that she and her henchwomen were becoming nothing but young waitresses to pass around the delectable sandwiches and cake that had come pouring in all day, much of it from people who hadn't been solicited at all. Hortense discovered that she had finally hit on something in the town that was really popular, yet nobody seemed to think that she had been the instigator. One elderly woman who had a wide smile and a pleasant sort of purr, came up to Hortense and said:

"Wasn't this a lovely idea, getting up this reception for Barney? Was it the Woman's Club did it, or the church? I suppose it must have been the church, because they all loved his mother so much. Though probably they all worked together."

Hortense was speechless with rage.

But finally the time came for the program, and Hortense assayed to take over. She got up on the platform, and patted her sparkling white hands with their many bright rings and their sharp crimson nails. She shouted as loud as her inadequate voice could be forced into shouting:

"Won't you all please come to order!" Then she patted her hands again, and fairly screamed at them. "Won't you all please come *to order.*"

Failing to get the attention of the noisy crowd she began to talk in a cross between a scream and a whine, until someone noticed her standing there, and said "Ssh!" and it hissed all over the room. There followed a lull in conversation. Then Hortense plunged in and tried to recite the speech she had prepared, but she suddenly forgot her lines, and stumbled and blundered around till the conversation began to buzz wildly around her again. Finally the young minister who had preached the night before, got up beside her, and with a voice that boomed out like a lovely trumpet he said:

"Friends, one of the committee is trying to call you to order and make an announcement."

There was instant silence, and he turned to Hortense for further facts, but Hortense was not going to surrender her rights so easily, and she began again to recite her piece:

"Friends, we are met together tonight to honor one of our number who has been out to fight for us, and has won great honors and come back to us with laurels on his brow. We have asked him to tell us about some of his great deeds, and how he won the purple heart and the silver star, and some of the other decorations he is wearing. We have also asked him to sing for us. I am turning over the program to our old friend and fellow-citizen Lieutenant Barney Vance. Lieutenant Vance."

Hortense's voice lisped along like a little chipping bird, and what she said wasn't heard over half the room at least, but when the end of the speech was reached, she made a sweeping bow toward Barney, and there was a tremendous cheer that shook the room till it seemed the roof would surely come down on them.

Then Barney, with a running jump, ascended the platform informally, grinning.

"Dear friends of my home town," he began, when the cheering had slowed down so he could be heard, "I do appreciate the welcome you have given me, and I do feel honored by your presence here. But as for the announcement about my speech, that was a mistake. I was asked to speak, yes, but I said no, until they told me I might sell war bonds. So, here goes. Who'll buy the first bond and start the ball a-rolling? What I did overseas was my part of the war. You don't need to know about that. Now this is the home front, and we want to sell a lot of bonds tonight to do our part, *here*. Who takes the first bond? That you, Mr. Haskell? How many? Miss Haskell, will you get a pencil and paper and sit right down here by the platform and make a record. Cy, you're from the bank, you take the money, and let's do this thing in an orderly way. Come, get to work, good people. Who's next? Ezekiel Summers, did I see your hand? One or two? Two? Put him down for two, Amelia."

The room grew very still listening to Barney Vance selling war bonds, and then it grew very enthusiastic as the sale went on and the sum of the bonds mounted up. They were really doing something big in Farmdale. They were really doing something big, weren't they? Something great for the war. And it was going over without the least assistance from Hortense, or without her being even recognized in connection with it. She was too vexed to take the frown off her brow and try to let on that she had done it all.

When the buying had reached the limit—a sum higher than any that had ever been subscribed in Farmdale before, for any cause—suddenly a prominent business man went up on the platform and looking straight at the handsome young soldier selling war bonds, called out: "Barney Vance, we were promised a song from you and we want to hear it now. My wife wasn't out to church Sunday morning but I told her all about that song you sung, the one about the Man on the throne of God offering His blood for the sins of us all, and I promised her if she could come tonight I'd ask you to sing it over again for her. Come on now, sing it, won't you? This will be a good time. Won't you sing it for my wife?"

Barney's face grew suddenly sober. He gave a quick look at the man, Mr. Harper, and then he glanced at the frowning Hortense, knowing that she wouldn't like it. But Hortense stood haughtily silent, as if she had not heard, and Barney turned back to Mr. Harper.

"Do you want that special song or would you like another?"

"I want that special song," said the man. "I thought that was *great.*"

"Very well," said Barney, gravely, "Margaret, where are you? Can you play it without the music?"

"Oh yes," she said, and went and sat down at the piano.

"The nerve of her!" whispered Hortense contemptuously.

Margaret's fingers touched the keys, quietly, almost reverently, and then Barney sang, with the instant attention a voice like his will always get.

"I see a Man at God's right hand,
Upon the throne of God,
And there in sevenfold light I see

The sevenfold sprinkled blood.
I look upon that glorious Man,
On that blood-sprinkled throne;
I know that He sits there for me,
That glory is my own."

The room was very still now. The words were going straight into hearts more even than they had done in the church, and it seemed that they were being understood. And then in the back of the room where Hortense had taken refuge when he began to sing, there was a movement. Quick, flashing, angry eyes brimming with frightened tears, and Hortense made a dive for the dressing room and disappeared from view. She fastened the door, too and no one saw the tears that pelted down over her make-up. Angry tears.

It may have been that Barney saw her go, sensed how disappointed she was, and felt somehow he ought to make it up to her in some way. He had prayed a little for her, but somehow he didn't seem to feel very genuine in his prayers. Too many years he had been growing in his distrust of her. Yet the Lord could forgive her, and love her, even though she was so silly and superficial. And if that was so he ought to be able to pray for her at least. Hadn't he seen tears in her eyes? Maybe somehow, a message had got across to her soul. The Lord was able to reach any soul.

But Hortense was not weeping for her sins, she was weeping for her*self*, and her own mortification in failing to get the admiration and acclaim from the whole community. She had wanted to show Barney what she could do, and to show those two upstarts of girls, and they had all simply been witnesses to her humiliation.

But Barney had little further time for thought about the silly girl, for he was surrounded by the old inhabitants of the home town, and he found that a reception could be a very pleasant affair when one knew the people well.

Hortense did not remain in the dressing room long to weep. She heard Barney's voice singing again, and knew that the song he was singing had been requested. That was a relief. She got out her make-up and repaired the damage done to her face, and then she went loftily out to resume her duties as hostess, and act exactly as if everybody knew that she had been responsible for this great social success. But she watched jealously the two girls who were so at home among these people, and the young man who was not giving her the attention that she felt he owed her now, since she had given him this reception.

But Barney was having a good time, and stayed willingly beyond the hour he had set as the time for his little company to retire from the social scene and go home. And when finally the company really began to break up, Barney went smilingly up to Hortense, shook her hand cordially, and thanked her for the pleasant evening she had planned for him. At least Hortense felt that she had been treated with outward respect, now at the end, even though Barney did frustrate every part of the program she had planned. Well, at least he had come, and done the courteous thing, and everybody had seen him do it. That somewhat salved her hurt feelings.

IT was the next morning that the telegram arrived from the admiral.

Roxy brought it up to him, reluctantly, because he had been up so late the night before and she thought he needed to sleep. But a telegram had always been an alarming thing to Roxy, so she finally decided it was her duty to let Barney be the judge.

A telegram? Barney was instantly wide awake and all attention. Yes, it was from the admiral. He blinked at it and began to read.

> If still interested in proposition be ready to start, awaiting telegram to come at once. You would have to be in Washington for medical examination first, and then await orders. Let me know your plans immediately.

Barney waited only a minute and then he sprang from his bed and went to the telephone, called up Western Union and sent his answer.

Still eager to go. Will be ready when you call. Gratefully yours,

Barney Vance.

After he had hung up the telephone it came to him that this was going to make a radical change in his program of the days. And first, he had to tell Margaret.

He knew that she was hoping against hope that her beloved would not have to go yet, on account of his health. He knew that she felt it was all wrong for him to have offered. If Stormy must be gone after, someone else surely ought to go, not Barney, who was himself but just out of the hospital, and not at all strong yet. And yet, she had been praying for Stormy's return, and he knew she was ready to give him a smiling farewell if he felt he must go.

Yes, he must tell Margaret now.

No, he couldn't tell her right away. She was in school. He couldn't disturb her until noon. Of course if he had to leave at once he wouldn't stop on that, but he didn't want a lot of curious children around when he told her. Of course he could call her on the telephone, but that would be hard on her. She would have to go back to her classes. No, there was no hurry yet. He would go down to the schoolhouse and be there when she came out to her lunch. They could walk a few steps together. Yet why was he making such a perplexity of this, for Margaret knew he wanted to go? She understood. And in a way she would be glad that he was getting his wish. Yet he knew what a trial it was going to be for her. And for himself too.

He drew a deep quivering sigh as he hurried with his dressing. Would this mean a long separation? Going after Stormy might not be quick work. It might be a long-drawn-out affair. And when he found him, *if* he did, would it perhaps involve imprisonment or even death for himself? Yes, he had counted the possibility of that when he first said he would go, but then he hadn't found Margaret yet. Now he had, and he saw that it was sorrow for her if that happened. He could well sacrifice himself for the man who had once saved his life, but to bring sorrow on his beloved was another matter. And yet he knew he could not back out, could not go back on his offer. Margaret knew about it and Margaret would not have him stay safely here when duty and loyalty called. Yes, it was going to be hard, but he *had* to go! Yes, and be *glad* over it, too. He must not be sad. That was no way to sacrifice, to do it sadly. No, he must trust God to bring it all out right.

But he went about his packing with a heavy heart. He had to own that it was not going to be easy to tell Margaret that he had practically received his summons. The admiral would not have sent that telegram if he hadn't been pretty sure that he had been able to put this thing across, and Barney was almost trembling at the thought of the trust that was being put in him. It seemed almost audacious in him to have suggested that he was fitted to go, and yet he had been so confident that he could find Stormy if he were allowed to try.

Very humble about it all he knelt down and talked to his Lord about it, and when he arose there was a new peace on his brow, also a certain assurance in his heart that Margaret would understand. It would be a sorrow they would have to bear together, but perhaps a special joy would come through that sorrow.

So it was with a grave face that he went downstairs and sought out Roxy, who had been filled with quiet forebodings ever since that telegram came.

"Well, Roxy," he said as he entered the kitchen and

saw the anxious face of his old nurse, "I guess I'm going to have my wish and be allowed to go after my lost friend."

"Oh, Mr. Barney! Now ain't that *awful!* They would never be letting you go if they knew how white you were still looking. I'm a mind to go myself down to Washington and *tell* them, so I am."

Barney grinned.

"No, Roxy, you mustn't think of that. They would only laugh at you and think you were an old mollycoddler. Besides, if they let me go I'll have to pass the doctor's test, so don't you worry. They won't let me go if I'm not able. And now see here, Roxy, you can't go around looking and acting like that. Don't you know God is managing this thing, and it can't go through unless He says so. We've done a lot of praying about this trip, and if I go I must go in the strength of the Lord, not my own strength. Besides, this isn't any worse than my going to war the first time, is it? And I came back, didn't I?"

"Well, there just doesn't seem any sense to it at all, you going through all that war, and being so sick and then getting back home, and having the temerity to go back again before you have to. It seems to me like tempting Providence."

"Oh, no, Roxy. It's not like that. I'm going of my own free will to try and find and bring back my friend who saved my life when he was wounded himself. You don't want me to be a coward, do you, Roxy?"

He talked for sometime to try and make her understand. All the time she was getting his breakfast and sitting around while he ate it, and then she was not more than half convinced that this was something his mother would have wanted him to do. Something that God wanted him to do or He would not have made it possible.

"Well, you aren't gone yet," she said at last. "Maybe

God'll stop it yet somehow. I think we need a bit more praying."

"Now Roxy," charged Barney, with a grin, "You wouldn't go and pray *against* me, would you?"

"No, not against you," said Roxy with a grim set of her lips. "I'll just pray that God will see to it that you behave till you get strong enough to go out saving people again."

Barney laughed and then went upstairs to put last things in his suitcase. If he should be called to go suddenly he must be ready. The admiral had asked that he do that. And it was getting almost time to go and meet Margaret. He mustn't miss that, and he would feel easier in his mind if the suitcase was ready to go whenever he left the house for a few minutes.

So he packed his things, for he had thought it all out in the night just what things would have to go to make him ready for any contingency he might have to meet. Then he went downstairs and smelled the cinnamon buns that Roxy was baking.

"Give me a couple, Roxy," he begged. "I'm going to meet Sunny at her lunch hour, and I thought if we had a couple of those nice hot cinnamon buns we could stay out a little longer, and she wouldn't have to go to the lunch room."

"Why of course," said Roxy brightening. "Here! I'll fix them in a little box for you."

In a trice she whisked four lovely candied buns rich with raisins into a box, with plenty of paper napkins to wipe off the stickiness afterwards.

Barney took the box and started away, trying to plan just how he would break the news to Margaret.

And then he didn't have to break it at all. Margaret understood at once. It seemed almost uncanny. She saw him as she came down the steps of the schoolhouse, and her eyes got wide with trouble.

"It's *come,*" she said breathlessly as she hurried to his side. "Hasn't it? Your summons has come, and they are going to let you go. Isn't that right? Please tell me quick and get it over with."

"You dear child!" was all Barney said, looking down at her with deep compassion in his eyes. "Perhaps I ought not to have suggested it. I didn't want *you* to have to suffer."

"No, it's all right, Barney! Truly it is! I want it to be God's way of course. But I've just been expecting this all day and when I saw you walking along with your shoulders over and your head bent I knew it must have come, and that you were realizing what it is going to be to us. But we're not the only people who have to suffer for this awful war, and of course we'll be brave and keep on praying."

"You dear child!" said Barney again, feeling sharp tears stinging into his eyes.

"Well, there!" said Margaret, giving a quick rub across her eyes. "That's over. Now tell me about it. What did they say? Were they pleased or not?"

"Here is the telegram," said Barney in a husky voice.

They stopped on the walk while Margaret read it, then she handed it back to him and looked up with a pale little watery smile.

"Well, I'm glad they didn't turn you down utterly. It shows they must have good reports of you, and they must think a lot of Stormy. Of you both of course. And I'm proud of you. It hurts, but I'm proud of you!"

Margaret's quiet sensible acceptance of the fact did a lot toward taking away the sting of the separation that was to come, the thought that perhaps he would never come back to her on this earth, when they had just found one another. But after they had walked quite a distance, and it was only a half hour before the school bell would sound for the afternoon session, they were calm enough to eat their cinnamon buns.

"Mmmm!" said Margaret eating the last crumb of hers. "They are good. I'm glad you brought them along. I'll thank Roxy for them myself the next time I see her."

"But think of all the time we wasted last night in that fool reception," said Barney. "When we might have been alone together."

"No!" said the girl cheerfully, "it wasn't wasted. I'm glad you had that reception, and glad I was in on it with you. It is something to remember while you are gone. Something beautiful. I shall always hear you singing to my heart, until you come back to sing to me again."

"Dearest!" said Barney, and stooped right on the public highway and kissed her.

"But Barney, dear, you *mustn't!* Can't you remember I'm the schoolma'am. They'll perhaps have me expelled for carrying on in public this way with a soldier! And there might be some of my bad boys around watching. And old lady Cramer lives in that little house up the road. They say she can see a mile away, and talk as if she had seven tongues."

And so they talked lightly, as if there were no anxieties and burdens in the world for them, and Barney went home almost cheered. What a wonderful girl she was! But he did not know that back in her little cloak room where she stored unused school books and boxes of chalk, and piles of old examination papers, Sunny was down on her knees behind an old blackboard asking for keeping for Barney, and strength for them both to go through this trial.

21

STORMY going down the dark river in a little open boat with a man who was supposedly fishing, lay under the great piece of sailcloth that was thrown carelessly over him, and now and again looked out furtively between the folds. He was trying to identify the places he was passing, cities he must have known well at one time. Yet some cities were so much alike at night it was hard to tell them apart. He feared even to think of names of places he knew, lest somehow the enemy might sense his thoughts. He knew nothing of the man in whose boat he traveled. He trusted nobody. He was only trying to follow orders. And lying still beneath that cover in the night he fell asleep.

Sometimes he wakened, but the cover was still upon him, and he lay as still as possible. He somehow felt he must not call the attention even of his fisherman.

He had carefully memorized all the papers he carried. If any enemies appeared he could destroy them and be little worse off than he was before when he had been in the underground.

He began to wonder about that radio, and if it would

be some new type that would make them suspect him. He tried to remember all he knew of such instruments that might be used on planes. He whiled away the long journey in that little boat by repeating over in his mind the names and numbers of the papers he carried. He must have these all at his tongue's end. There must be no hesitation in his answers if any questions were asked.

In the dimness of the dawning they reached the airport, a bleak place with no lights, and hazy ships like giant shadowy insects hovered about in most unexpected places.

The oarsman who had been strangely silent all the way drew up to land, pointed to a distant building dimly outlined against the dawn and uttered one single word, "Hangar." Then he took away the covering cloth and helped his passenger to get out, which was not an easy job after such a long time of lying in one cramped position. His feet on solid ground again he watched his conductor turn his boat and sweep away into the dimness from which they had come. Just like that, without a word! Twelve hours at least he must have been in the company of that man, and they had not spoken to each other, save that one word. Stormy would not know him if he were to see him in the daylight. Would he ever see him again? Was he a saved man or an enemy perhaps? That might of course be possible. For it would not have been easy to get a native to bring him here.

But now he had no time to think. His orders were to go at once to the office and report. He took out his identification papers and walked with as firm a step as he could muster with the stiffness in his legs. It was well that it was still dark or his gait might be noticeable.

The man in the office was asleep, his head down on his folded arms upon the desk, and Stormy had to pound on the door to waken him and gain admittance, and attention.

He stood waiting while the official read his papers with sleepy eyes, and then looked him over, saying a few words in French, to the effect that he was the new radio operator to take the place of the man who had been taken sick. It was well for Stormy that he had been well taught in languages and could converse easily in several, so he had no trouble in answering the few questions.

The official showed him where to go, and what would be required of him, told him it was uncertain when the plane would leave, assigned him temporary quarters where he could rest till the day officer would arrive who would give him further orders. Then he departed, and Stormy lay down on the hard cot in the bare little room and shivered. The broken rest, the bleakness of the airport, the dismal outlook into a day in which a fine drizzle of rain was obscuring the surroundings, combined to make him feel half sick. But he was a soldier and not expecting luxury. And he was on his way. A few mouthfuls of the dry bread he had brought with him, and a swallow or two of water from a pitcher on the shelf, a bit of a prayer, and he felt better, and went off into a refreshing sleep.

The day officer seemed more indifferent than the night officer had been, and it struck Stormy that all the people he saw coming and going about that airport, looked unhappy, and suspicious, as if they trusted nobody. But he did not venture to talk with any except when he had to ask a question about his duties. He judged that as this was enemy occupied territory none dared to trust any, and so he did not do so himself. He was glad that nobody asked him questions. They did not seem to care whence he came, or whither he was going. Each went his way with sodden indifference.

He was clothed as inconspicuously as possible, having got rid of the ragged enemy-uniform he had worn when he escaped from the camp. The little parking room where they had put him when he came contained a coat and cap evidently worn by the former radio operator, now sick. Stormy appropriated them. They were a bit too small, but what did that matter? They seemed clean and gave him a more self-respecting look.

The three days of waiting went hard with Stormy, and as he began to experiment with the radio he wished he dared send some message to his outfit, but the friend who had helped him at the underground had warned him not to try anything like that. He must remember that he was still in enemy-occupied territory.

At last the time of waiting was over, and the plane appeared. Then there was work to do, messages to be sent, and by this time he was fairly well acquainted with his instrument. He was filled with excitement to think that in a little while now he would be out of enemy-oc-cupied land and free to go on where he would. But he had been trained in a hard school and well knew that he must not count on anything ahead. Almost anything might happen yet to hold him up. And he prayed that it might not be too long for the information of which he was possessed to be of value.

That last night before the plane came he slept but fitfully and often in his dreams he saw that vision again that had been with him during the fever. That angel with the face of a girl, that girl he had seen at camp back in his home land. The girl whose tiny snapshot collected from among her brother's pictures the last time he was back with the outfit had gone with him everywhere so far, hidden inside the pocket of his blouse, where happily no sneering guard had yet discovered it. It was only a tiny one, and now soiled and crumpled in spite of his care, but somehow that face had cheered him when he felt utterly without human friends. Could it be that he would see that girl herself some day? That there was hope he might yet go home and see her? Her brother Jim had been his friend. There might be an opportunity. It was a pleasant hope to ponder on as he watched the great plane come sailing into the airport. Only a figment of his imagination, perhaps, but it helped to pass the time away.

Then things began to happen. He was given many messages to send, some that contained facts that he knew his officers back at the outfit would be glad to get. Some that he would fain have withheld from sending to the enemy. Dared he do a bit of editing? He wished he could, but he must run no risks for the sake not only of himself but for the sake of those good people who had taken their lives in their hands to help to set him free. He had been warned.

As he set sail at last out into the gloomy world a great exultation filled him. He was *going*.

How he wished he were free to replace that pilot up there, and drive that plane where he would. For he was a pilot himself of course and felt at home in the air. If only there had been nobody but himself and the pilot on board, he could easily have overpowered the pilot and taken over. But there were a lot of people on board, soldiers of course, and sturdy men. And anyway he should not think such crazy thoughts. For while under certain circumstances he might have gotten away with it, it would certainly have reacted on those blessed people of the underground who had helped him away, and were living to help others who might escape, and he could think of nothing more despicable than to be disloyal to them.

Still there was exhilaration in being among the clouds

again and daring to hope that in the not far distance he might be seeing his buddies of the outfit, and be perhaps hearing from home. Again he wondered about Barney Vance. Where was he? Was he living yet, and did he get well and go home, or was he still in a hospital bed, as he had left him.

And that was the morning that Barney received that first telegram from the admiral.

The first airport was passed at last. The next one was still many miles ahead. Stormy's heart was pounding in his breast as they went on. Soon, soon though they would pass out of enemy jurisdiction. The second airport! There the new radio man was to take over and he would be free to edge along into unoccupied territory.

It was only a little while after that that he noticed something queer about the way they were flying, something quite out of the ordinary. He wished he dared go over to that pilot and suggest something. He wished he dared take over to run them into safety. He felt fairly certain he knew what was the matter with that plane, but that wasn't his business, and might of course lay him open to suspicion. He must not do that. If he should be taken prisoner, here, now, before they had crossed the border into free land what would become of all the valuable information he carried in his mind. It would be lost to his side, he would probably be taken prisoner again, too. No, he must be quiet and calm.

"Oh, God, take over, please!" he prayed.

And now the plane was definitely out of hand, and going down swiftly, a forced landing was inevitable. Stormy looked down. Was that water beneath those clouds, or mountains, or what? He couldn't see for the rain and mist that surrounded the swiftly falling ship. The passengers were in a panic. He could easily have been in one himself, to have to come down among the enemy when he had been almost out into freedom. Was God going to let this happen to him again? Was this what He had planned? But if it was going to happen of course it was in the eternal plan, and Stormy must yield in contentment.

"Oh God, take over for me. I can do nothing myself," he prayed.

And then the crash came!

22

BARNEY had waited five days for another message from the admiral before it came. A day letter sent that morning making an appointment in Washington.

Barney was all ready to go, although he had about lost hope that he would hear anything more of his request. He took only time for a brief telephone conversation with Margaret, and hurried on his way to Washington, leaving a deeply disappointed Roxy, weeping salt tears into her dishpan, and a bright-haired girl who had already shed her tears, and had prayed her way through to peace, trying to smile through her day of hard work in school.

Meanwhile Barney was on the train, trying to forget the sad little lilt of his dear girl's voice as she bade him God-speed and told him how she would be praying all the time for him.

They hadn't had much time to talk, for he knew he should catch the first train possible, and he knew also that she had duties which he must not interrupt. Besides, they had said good-by last night, with always the thought every night that perhaps he might have to go before she saw him again.

But presently he was able to turn his attention to what might be just before him.

He got out his telegram and read it over carefully. Oh, it was all uncertain business. He wished he could have gone straight from his hospital before he came home. That would have been the way to find Stormy. All this endless delay! And now, he would scarcely know which direction to take, unless the outfit had since received more definite knowledge of where Stormy had been taken prisoner.

He put his head back on the seat and closed his eyes, trying to pray. He was in God's hands, why should he be so upset by a simple change of plans? God was in Washington. He was across the seas. He knew whether it was in the plan for Barney to go after Stormy or not. Why should he fret? And so, laying down his burden, peace came to his heart and he slept.

One of the hardest things in life for Barney to do was to wait patiently for something he wasn't in the least sure of, and he found that there was a good deal of that in store for him for the next two days. Then suddenly things began to happen.

The admiral's secretary came to him in the office where she had parked him the day before, and sent him off to the doctor to have a thorough physical examination.

Barney saw in that only another way to hinder him for he knew he was not up to his normal strength yet, and he did not want that held up against him. He knew that he *could* go out and fight again if he was back with his companions and that was his duty. He knew that he had strength enough to do what he had set out to do under ordinary circumstances, or even under extraordinary ones. And even if it was not the way to recover normal strength now, yet we were at war, weren't we? And soldiers were not expected to consider themselves. Still he felt he was fit enough and would be all right, and if the Lord wanted him to go he was going. That is if the army would let him. And of course if he was allowed to go that would be a sign that it was the Lord's will. But he went to the doctor as he was ordered, waited an unconscionable time for his turn, answered innumerable questions, and got very little personal satisfaction out of the interview, save that he was advised that he still needed to take as much rest as possible. Then he went back to the admiral's secretary, and was told that the admiral would see him the next morning, and hoped to have definite information for him.

Meanwhile Barney had taken all this waiting time to write a letter to Margaret, a real love letter, the first he had ever written, pouring out all the precious thoughts of his heart for her, trying to make up for the brief time they had had together since they had found out their love.

Dear Sunny:

You will not mind if I use the dear name I knew first, will you, my darling, in this my first love letter to you? It somehow seems right that I should bridge the years in this way.

My precious love, you cannot know how hard it has been to leave you this way, when we have but just found each other. And yet I think you understood that it meant an obligation which could not be ignored. I think, too, that you agreed with me that it was right for me to go. But that is something we have talked over, something that we have left in the Lord's hands, and both of us are trusting that He will bring it out in His own way.

But now I want to go back to the first morning when I returned from overseas, and saw you standing down among the apple blossoms, your sweet face looking up to the bird singing by my window.

I am astonished at myself that I haven't told you this before, but we had so little time alone you know, and there were so many important things to say. I wanted this to be a very special time, this telling you the lovely picture you made there among the apple blossoms, when you didn't even know I was there watching you. So I'm going to take this first minute by myself, when I've nothing to do but think about you, and this seems the best way to feel near to you, by bringing out that dear picture I have in my very recent memory. When I woke this morning I took a look at it as I always do every morning since I first saw you, and I feel guilty that I have not told you about it before.

But now, I am wondering if I can find words to paint the picture of you as I saw you that morning when the birds were singing, and I was at home again after war and horror, and pain and desolation.

It was the time of the singing of birds, you know, and they were fairly whooping it up out there in the apple tree, that was all pink and white blossoms, with sunshine glinting through the perfumed air.

And then I heard the soft crunch of wheels on the gravel of the drive, blending into my dreams, but scarcely noticed it as anything out of harmony with the waking world, till suddenly I heard a silver sweet whistle, high and clear, a whistle that I had thought for years was practically my personal property. Astonished I listened, and there it came again.

This I have told you before, briefly, of course, and have since heard you give a demonstration of what you can do in that line. But that night was so suddenly interrupted that I did not tell you what was in my heart, and somehow there has never been a time since when I could return to it, because there were so many other important things to say.

Barney took time and much comfort in describing the thrill that came to him with the silver sound of Sunny's whistle, and smiled as he set down the lovely words of description, almost as if he were writing notes in a musical score.

And then he came to the picture as he went to the window and saw her.

He was like an artist taking out his tubes of paint and arranging them on his palette, mixing and blending them to express just the right shade of meaning as he gathered out the words and set them in order in his mind, till it resolved itself into a delight to put them into the picture.

So the letter grew and went on to almost a volume.

Oh, it wasn't all a love letter! There were bits of incidents he had met by the way as he walked about the streets of Washington. There were notable people to mention and describe, some he had even met, and there were items of war news that perhaps hadn't yet got on the radio. He described some of the great buildings he had visited to pass the time away, told of the lovely flowers in the parks. And then he went back to his love for Margaret and began to tell her all over again how happy it made him that she loved him, so happy that he couldn't rightly think about the serious mission he was expecting presently to go out on. A mission that would probably be filled with peril and danger and toil and weariness before he could even hope to come back to her, if he *ever* came. But he did not want to make her suffer as he was suffering every time he thought of that possibility.

Two or three times Barney came on lovely little things that he could send back to his dear girl. A charming bracelet, delicately wrought. A few pictures of the city. Other souvenirs. He wanted to get her a ring as soon as there was time. As soon as he could get back to her, and put it on her hand himself. It was too sacred a thing for him to do by "absent treatment," he told himself.

But thinking about that matter of a ring brought back the memory of the day when his mother took off her engagement ring. It was getting too tight for her, and she had to work for some time before she could slip it off. He remembered that he had finally gone and helped her.

"I shall likely never wear it again," she had said, with a sigh and the quick flashing of a smile at the end that he knew was put there for him. She was studying these days to leave no sad memories for him. He had had flashes of understanding of this at times, in those days, but he had been so filled with eagerness over his own approaching entrance into the army that he didn't fully realize. Now, however, it came to him fully, to understand and realize what that scene with the ring had meant to his mother. She was saying good-by to him forever. That is, so far as this earth was concerned.

Now he felt that he must review it thoroughly and understand everything, come nearer to his mother in knowing what this all had meant to her. She must have known that she would not be here when he came back.

It had been a bright lovely day, almost the first of May, and the birds were singing then, just as they were singing now. As he thought of it their shrill sweet voices seemed hopelessly tangled with that look of pain on his mother's face. That sweet quiet sacrifice of all that she counted dear because she knew that the cause for which he was going forth to fight was a cause of righteousness, and loyalty to his country. Freedom and Right were calling him. It was God's cause and God would care for him. That was the way his mother had felt.

And she had taken off that old blue ring, a sapphire it was, an *old* sapphire, as if she were giving up the self she had been through the years. She had told him about the ring again that day, although he remembered she had often spoken of its history before. She had said it was worth a great deal of money. He wondered if that could possibly be true. Valuable? Why would a simple blue stone be valuable? It wasn't even a star sapphire was it? Just a blue stone. A sapphire. Was that a precious stone, or just a semi-precious one? But his mother had always spoken of it as something very unusual. Would she know about such things? Her grandfather had brought it home with him from some far land, he couldn't remember the story, but it was written down somewhere. His mother had put the story in the box with the ring, and told him that he was to get it reset and give it to his bride some day.

He had laughed when she gave it to him, and said that he hadn't any idea of getting married, and it would be a long time before he did if he went to war, before he had time to get acquainted with any girls. She had kissed him as she put the ring box in his hand and told him she hoped he would find the right girl, and never give her ring into the keeping of a girl who was not worthy of him. He wondered as he remembered this if possibly his mother hadn't been thinking of Hortense when she said this. How she had always dreaded Hortense's coming! He had not then understood that in his sweet gentle loving mother—to be so set against one girl that she couldn't see anything good in her at all. But now, since he had been at home and had seen more of Hortense's machinations, he could understand. Mother had looked into the girl's character when she was quite young and had seen what she was. Wise dear mother! Oh, could mother see dear Sunny, his precious lovely Margaret now? Surely if she knew, she was happy over his having found her. He seemed to feel that he had his mother's blessing on this union he hoped would come about some day—if he lived to come home.

He thought about the blue ring again. Would Margaret like it? He must find out whether she liked it or not before he gave it to her. Or rather could he offer it as a substitute for a diamond, until he could get home and really pick out the stone she liked best? Why hadn't he done something about that ring before he left home? She could have been wearing it while he was away, a sort of a bond between them till he returned. It was too late to do it now of course, for the blue ring was in the bank with all his valuable papers. And there was another thing he ought to have done. He should have made a will and left everything to Margaret. That was what should be of course, and perhaps he could find a lawyer here in Washington and arrange that, having the paper sent to the bank afterward. Yes, he must look after that. He could even arrange that by telephone, probably. No, he would have to sign papers of course. But he just must not forget that. One couldn't be too careful when one was going into a dangerous zone, and while money of course was not greatly important, still he would like to have his go to his dear girl, if anything happened to him.

But if he did get back home soon he must go and get that ring and examine it carefully, have it appraised, and then ask Margaret if she liked it. If she knew the story of its being his mother's she would be likely to ask to have it in place of any other ring, for she loved his mother, and would be prejudiced in its favor, but he would not speak of what his mother had said until he really found out if she liked it. He would not condemn her to wear something the rest of her days that she perhaps had disliked.

So he planned, and filled his time of waiting with pleasant thoughts.

He had a little snapshot of Margaret that he had begged last Sunday night, and kept it in a little leather case in his pocket over his heart. Often he would take it out and look into that sweet face, and remember how beautiful she was, and how wonderful it was that God had kept such a lovely girl safe for him until he could get home to find her. Surely God would let him come back again to her. "Oh my Father, keep her safely!" he prayed in his heart again and again as he went about through those days of waiting before he expected to leave.

And so as he lay down to rest that last night before he was to meet the admiral and get some definite answer about his request, he was thinking of Margaret—Sunny as he still called her in his most intimate thoughts—and feeling that she was very near. She was probably kneeling now to pray for him, for they had arranged a trysting hour for prayer which he meant to keep whenever possible, even if it meant amid battle or danger. So was somewhat dispelled the anxiety which he had been feeling about the outcome of the morrow.

About a half hour before it was time to go to the admiral's office Barney was ready, and sat glancing over the morning paper, noting the headlines and what had been happening overnight in the war zones, when he heard footsteps coming along the hall. Could it be the bell boy bringing up another telegram? Oh, he hoped there was not going to be another long delay. Well, if there was to be, and he had to go back home, he would at least try to do something about that ring, so that Margaret would have something to help her feel he was hers.

And then the footsteps paused outside his door!

But instead of knocking a hand took hold of the knob and turned it, the door opened, and there stood Stormy Applegate!

23

BARNEY took a deep breath and passed his hand over his eyes. Was he seeing things? He must have high blood pressure or something. This couldn't be real. This tall soldier who looked so much like Stormy, only somehow thinner, and tired-looking, who stood there in his doorway grinning at him. He *couldn't* be Stormy. Why they didn't even know for certain that Stormy was alive yet, and if he was he must be on the other side of the world!

"Stormy!" he gasped. "My word, man, is it really you? How did you manage to get here? Why—we thought you were *lost!* We didn't even know whether you were alive or not. They all said you weren't, but I wasn't letting it go at that. I was sure you were alive, and I have been doing my best to get permission to go out and hunt you up."

"I know," grinned Stormy. "I heard about that, but I *beat you to it!* I didn't want you to take all that trouble when I was having to come anyway you see, so I just caught the next plane after I'd imparted the information I was sent for, and here I am! Glad to see me, old man?"

"Glad to see you?" said Barney springing to his feet and

grasping Stormy's hand. "Glad to see you? *I'll say* I am! Bless the Lord for bringing you through!"

"Amen!" said Stormy heartily.

And then suddenly Barney felt weak in the knees and as if all the happenings of the last two weeks had got him down.

"Sit down," he said grasping Stormy's arm and pressing him into the big chair by the window. "Tell me all about it. Where have you been and how did you get here?"

"Well, that's a pretty big order, Barn," said the other man, "but I imagine I can sketch out a kind of an outline of my doings if I take the rest of the day. Got plenty of time?"

"Oh," said Barney, suddenly remembering the admiral and his engagement. "No, I forgot. I've got an engagement in two minutes now with the admiral and I'll have to run. Come with me, won't you? He's the one who has been arranging for me to go over after you, and he told me he would give me a definite answer this morning."

"That's all right," grinned Stormy, waving Barney off as he tried to draw him to his feet, "*I'm* the definite answer. I just came from your admiral, and he sent me over to tell you, you needn't come till five o'clock this afternoon, and we are to take dinner with him at his house tonight, so settle down and relax and I'll begin my story."

"But—did the admiral know all the time that you were coming?"

"Well, no, not *all* the time. But he knew day before yesterday. He's been cabling like mad to the outfit, and when they got my first contact, which was as soon as I could get to a telephone in unoccupied territory after the crash—"

"Crash?" asked Barney excitedly. "Were you back in combat?"

"No, I was on my way out of occupied territory, and we had a crash a few miles before we escaped from there. It was just a mere trifle of something like fifty or a hundred miles, and no way to get over the line but to *walk,* and dodge bombs and incidental snipers, but at last I got to a friendly town and found a telephone, and let them know I was alive. I couldn't give them much information of course. Too important, but I called my officer and told him number two question of our list was as he hoped, and that was the most important question I was sent to find out. Then I said I'd get there as soon as I could get transportation, for walking was almost too slow, not while I had valuable information to impart. So they maneuvered a plane after me, and I got there at last and gave my report. Then they told me you were out after me, and had been keeping the wires hot in pursuit, so they sent me through a medical exam and then got me a plane over here, so here I am!"

"Praise the Lord!" said Barney, his face shining. "But—tell me about the crash. How did it happen? Where was it? Were you hurt? Was anybody hurt?"

"Not so fast. You know I've been through a nervous shock and I can't answer everything at once. The crash was pretty bad, and I don't know how long I was unconscious, but pretty soon I felt it getting pretty hot and I woke to consciousness, and found the plane was on fire. Then I got busy. A good many were killed, and only a few of the passengers were able to crawl out. I managed to get out. But it was a long time before I got to anywhere, and I guess some of the men that escaped the fire died before help came. But you know how such things are. You've been through enough yourself."

"Indeed I have."

"Well, Jim Mayberry wanted to take a plane back to look up the people that were saved in the crash, but he was needed in another direction and went by himself to get some more information. He's beginning to do some notable things along that line now. Bright kid he is."

"Yes," said Barney. "I thought that when I was there, but he's a quiet fellow. It wasn't easy to know him well, but I got to like him a lot. And by the way I think he has accepted the Lord."

"He *has?* That's wonderful! I hoped he would come to see it. You know you can't go around in the face of death continually and not see yourself, and see what the Lord can do, and how much everybody needs Him."

"That's right," said Barney. "I had several quiet talks with Jim while I was still in the hospital. He's never had much teaching along those lines, and has had to think things out for himself, but it seems to me that one meets God out there among flying bombs and learns directly from Him, and perhaps that's the best way to know God, and to see oneself."

The two young men were silent for a moment, enjoying the quiet agreement of fellowship they were having. Then Barney said:

"Did you know Jim's sister was over here, in Farmdale visiting her aunt? She's been much interested in you, by the way, been one of our group who were praying that you might be found."

Stormy looked up with quick interest:

"She *has?*" he said, greatly stirred. "I met her once in camp before we left this country. I didn't suppose she'd remember me."

"She *does,*" said Barney. "She asked me one day if you were a Christian. She is greatly interested in the subject. She seemed to feel that it would be very terrible if you had died without knowing the Lord. You see everybody had told her that you were probably killed. Even Jim wrote her that was the general opinion of the outfit. And she was greatly concerned to know if you were saved. Things of the kingdom have become very real to her these days. She has told us that she knows you."

Stormy was silent searching the face of his friend. At last he asked slowly, quietly, *"You* are then interested in her?"

"Me? Interested in Cornelia Mayberry? No, not specially, except that I have tried to tell her more about the Lord in answer to her questions now and then, but our conversation has been mainly about you. It seems that she remembers you very vividly."

"That's strange," said Stormy, "we had scarcely any opportunity to talk together, just a little fun now and then when everybody was by. But I have thought often of her, and wished I knew if she had ever found the Lord. She was a most interesting girl."

"Yes," said Barney. "She is intimate with a dear friend of mine, and so I have seen her rather often since I have been at home. But that hasn't been so long you know."

"No, it hasn't been long as the world counts time, since you and I parted and went our way to meet death, yet here we are and it seems that years must have passed. What has the time brought to you, fella? Changes? I remember they said your mother had died. That will have made it hard for your homecoming."

"Yes, it has," said Barney, "but she expected it and wrote me a farewell letter left in her desk. It gave me courage to go on. I had time to write her before she went how I had come to know the Lord intimately, and she was so glad of that. She has left me the feeling that she's just over at the gate of Heaven waiting for me till I get done with my work here, and that we must not either of us mourn, because we're meeting soon."

"How precious to have a heritage like that!" said Stormy, and then he sighed. "I never really knew my mother at all. She died when I was just a little chap, and my father didn't live much longer. He was killed in the last war. I was raised by a lot of relatives who didn't quite understand me, and now think I am a fanatic. It doesn't matter of course, but it would have been pleasant to have had a mother and a father. Barney, how has it seemed, getting back to real living again? Or is it real living? Sometimes I have thought the real part was over there where we see the stark side of life and everybody is on a level before God."

"It is, isn't it!" said Barney. "I think we didn't understand what life was for before we went into battle."

"That's right," said Stormy. "But how has it seemed, coming back? Have you been happy, fella?"

Then suddenly Barney looked up and his face was illuminated by a great smile, the smile that Sunny called his "golden look."

"Why yes, Stormy, I've been happy! Very happy! I was coming to that. God has given me a great joy. The love of the most wonderful girl I have ever known. I never knew there was any earthly joy like that! Of course we've only known this a comparatively few days, but I've practically known her all my life. She was just a little kid when I went away to college, but now she's grown into a beautiful woman, as lovely of soul as she is of face, but wait till you see her. Her name is Margaret Roselle, and her mother was one of my mother's dearest friends. She and I have been praying for you that you might come home. Stormy, I only hope some day you'll know a love like this."

Stormy was silent again, but his face had a glorified interest in it.

"I'm glad for you," he said. "I thought there was

something new about you, something that was making you very glad. I thought perhaps at first when you said you had found a girl that it might be Jim's sister. Jim talked a good deal about her."

"Well, she's a very wonderful girl," said Barney. "Margaret enjoys her a lot. They are awfully good friends. They seem to be most congenial. But wait till we get home and you'll see."

"Yes," said Stormy eagerly, "I'm looking forward to that. I'm looking forward to meeting your girl, too. She's got to be something very special to satisfy me for you, Barney."

"She *is,*" said Barney with his glorified smile again. "And then," he added, "you'll like Cornelia, I'm sure you will. And you've got to remember that she's *very much* interested in you. In fact, she has a picture of you that she cherishes. It's a snapshot her brother gave her I think, but she showed it to me and asked if you had changed any."

Stormy listened eagerly, thoughtfully.

"Do you know," said he slowly, "I'm interested in her too. And I have a picture of her. I made Jim give it to me just before I went away that last time. I've carried it with me wherever I've gone. It's been a sort of mascot. I don't know what she would think if she knew I had it, but sometimes I've taken it out and looked at it, and it has helped me over hard places. Queer, isn't it, to take over an almost stranger and let her be a help in loneliness, because one didn't have any folks of one's own. But it has really meant a lot to me. Sometime perhaps I'll know her well enough to apologize for having taken the liberty, but anyway it's been good. I hope she won't be angry with me for presuming—if I ever tell her."

Barney looked at Stormy joyously.

"She won't be angry," he said, "and *you'll tell her* of

course. Wait till we get to Farmdale. Why did the admiral want to see us? Why invite us to dinner? I'd rather get home and tell Margaret what's happened. And tell Cornelia, too."

"Yes," said Stormy, "I would too, but your admiral was so insistent that we come, and he said there were some of the people who had been assisting him about your request who wanted to see us. I think we should go. He said they wanted to ask some questions. You know, the old dope that you have to give over the radio every little while, perhaps. Anyhow he's been so kind to us both we'll have to go of course."

"Of course," said Barney, "but I wish we could hurry away right off. I want to see Margaret, and I want you to see Cornelia."

Stormy sat for a moment in silence, thoughtfully. Then he spoke, as if it was something he must explain.

"I have had the strangest experience about Cornelia," he said. "Sometimes I wonder if I was out of my head when it happened. I guess perhaps I was at one time at least. I had been going for days with scarcely anything to eat, chewing a little dried grass, once a raw egg I found in a deserted shack, and once a can of tomatoes. Then so long a time with nothing, not even any clean water to drink. I had a fever I know, and couldn't think very straight. I thought I had reached the end and I was dying, and then there came a spot of moonlight and I saw her face, like an angel, up by the clouds. I wasn't rational enough to work it out the first time who she was, just an angel that God had sent to cheer me, to help me to Heaven perhaps. And looking at her face I fell asleep. I saw her face several times after that, and when I began to come to myself I took out her picture and looked at it. I saw they were the same."

He took out the little picture, looked at it earnestly, and then handed it over to Barney.

"Does she look like that now?" he asked.

"Yes," said Barney taking the picture. "Exactly."

There came a satisfied look in Stormy's eyes, and then he met Barney's glance with a grin:

"You think I'm a *nut,* don't you?" he said.

But Barney grinned back.

"No," said Barney, "I don't! Besides, you see, I'm in love myself, and I know what it is to be lonely and long for someone to act like homefolks."

"Yes, I guess that's it," said Stormy half sheepishly. "But I'll be glad to get to Farmdale. Of course she'll think I'm a fool I suppose. She's from a swell family, all kinds of money and social training and all that, but I want to see her, anyway. Maybe I won't feel this way when I see her in the flesh again, but I've got to get this idea out of my system before I'll be much good anywhere."

"Oh, *sure!* You've got it *bad!*" grinned Barney. "I know the symptoms. I haven't got over them yet myself. After all I've had such a few days with Margaret."

"Well, come on you old bomber, it's time we went and got some lunch. I'll own I'm hungry as a bear. I've not been in the land of plenty so long but that I get hungry now and then. And after lunch, two o'clock to be more accurate, I promised that you and I would appear at that radio station and give a broadcast of our life together in service. Something about the camp life and how I was supposed to have saved your life, and how you tried to save mine or something along those lines. Though of course we won't. We'll just shy off politely and sneak out. But we've got to appear once for I promised. It was all the fault of that doggone admiral. If he hadn't been right there on tiptoe, smiling, I would have got out of it somehow, but he seems to think he's running mamma's two little boys, and we have to do whatever he chooses to order next."

So they went to lunch, then to the radio station, then walked a little about the city seeing a few things they hadn't seen before. They brought up at the admiral's stately mansion and were ushered into the presence of the entire body of powers who had under their control such matters as the request of Barney that he might go out and hunt for Stormy.

It was an august body, and most impressive, and Stormy grinned to himself to think that these dignified gentlemen could have any conception of what it had been like to get lost out there. To roll out of an internment camp between barbed wires, to go hungry for days. And not knowing that, how could they presume to order whether a lost one should be searched for, or allowed to stay lost? Also he thought how good it was to know that God Himself was able to order matters over the heads of all the notables in any country, and work out the need of every living soul.

But the men were interesting and pleasant. They took a personal interest in the two young men who had made such attainments in war service. The dinner was good, the conversation a bit thrilling because it smacked of political problems, and deadly differences of opinion, and it gave Barney and Stormy an opportunity to get the pulse of their country at first hand, as it was represented by a few of the powerful men who had the affairs of the country in their hands, at least for the time being.

After dinner they went into a great luxurious library and sat around a costly table. They answered a lot of questions, that at first seemed utterly pointless, but afterward it developed that these two young men were to be appointed heads of a new group which should function for the furtherance of an understanding of the enemy, what enemy plans were likely to be and how to frustrate them.

It appeared that these two because of their valor in bombing enemy planes, and in searching in dangerous places for valuable information, were to be awarded notable honors. They were told to return to Washington on a certain day in the near future to publicly receive these awards. They were also informed that after their furloughs were ended they would be assigned to new work which likely would keep them in Washington, or vicinity at least for some time.

Dazed, almost bewildered the two young men went back to their hotel room at last and sat down to discuss the matter for awhile, and then side by side they knelt and committed it all to their heavenly Father. And then as it was definite orders and not anything that they had a choice about, they went to bed. They were still in the army and what the army said, they must do.

"Well," said Barney, "I can't help thinking there may be good in it. I'm not anxious to go on killing, or even spying, but I'm entirely willing to teach others the methods by which I gained my honorable mentions."

"Yes," said Stormy, "this war isn't going on forever of course, and I guess it's our turn to have a little look at peace before we leave and go up higher."

So the next morning they went home to Farmdale, having first telephoned Roxy to have a good dinner ready, and told her to please invite Margaret and Cornelia to dinner that night.

"It's a surprise," said Barney, "Roxy won't tell, but she'll see that the girls are there and that there is plenty to eat, but they won't know a thing yet about you being home, nor our new status in the army."

So like two little boys planning mischief, these two tall handsome soldiers plotted to relax and have a little fun.

Meantime the two girls back in Farmdale prayed most earnestly, wondering if Barney had started for overseas yet, and how many weeks it would be before they would hear from him, and know what he had been able to do.

Hortense and her crowd were wondering what was going to happen next and how they could manage to reap a little benefit from that reception they had put over on the unsuspecting Barney. Wondering what they should do next to separate him from those two obnoxious girls who seemed to have absorbed him.

"We might have a religious service in the public square," said Hortense. "Sunday afternoon would be a good time and get an enormous crowd. And we could get up a glee club and sing choruses and songs. We could decorate the platform in the park with flags, and get a band, and let them play softly all through the prayer,—I suppose we'd *have* to have a prayer, wouldn't we? We couldn't get by without that, could we, not with Barney in it, for if we didn't have it on the program he'd drag one in somehow. I never saw what a religious complex that fellow has! I declare it's a shame. He simply spoils everything we try to get up."

"Well, what I don't understand is, why you insist upon working Barney into everything," said Janet Harper. "He isn't our kind, you *know* he isn't, and you can't make him over, no matter how hard you try. If I were you I'd go down to the camp and get some soldiers who *aren't* that kind, soldiers who'll be real peppy and ready for any devilment you want to get up, and then you can have some real fun."

"Well, to tell you the truth," said Hortense wearily, "there aren't hardly any of that other kind left. They seem to all have got soft and religious. I can't understand it. Just as soon as they get into real fighting they seem to get awfully religious. Do you know, the other night at the canteen, where I was helping to entertain soldiers, a kid walked in and the hostess asked him if he would like to dance. He said no, he didn't know how to dance. And she said: Oh, that's all right. You go right up those stairs and you'll find a woman up there who will *teach* you to dance, and you can come back down here and have a real good time. It doesn't take her long to teach you a few steps. And do you know that fellow fairly glared at her, and he was only a kid, too. But he said, 'Lady, I didn't come in here to learn how to dance. I've got to go out tomorrow morning into battle and be ready to *die* perhaps, and I came in here to find somebody who could teach me how to die.' Did you ever hear of such talk? Can you imagine it? Talking like that to really nice people who were trying to help him have a little good time? Why it made me positively *sick* when I heard it. I didn't want to stay there any longer where a thing like that could happen. I hate all this talk about dying. Everybody has to die sometime I suppose of course, but I certainly don't want to hear about it till my time comes."

"Well, Hortense, if you wait till your time comes," spoke up Hank suddenly, "it will certainly be too late to get ready to die. But perhaps you don't care. Probably you think you can get by without getting ready."

"Oh, shut up," said Hortense. "Are you getting religious too? I declare, if you are, I'm off you for life!"

"Well, I wouldn't be losing so much at that," said Hank sourly. "All I get out of this is a chance to do your heavy work. If I'd quit you I might have a little time left on my hands, and I'd stand some chance of learning myself how to die. They tell me I'm in line to be called to war pretty soon, and I might need to know."

"It's a pity you wouldn't try a little religion yourself, Hortense," said Janet Harper. "You might be able to get hold of Barney that way. You've tried everything else on him and it doesn't work, but I think he'd be caught that way."

"Oh, for Pete's sake! What's the matter with you all?" said Hortense angrily, and walked off with her chin up and her eyes flashing angrily.

24

THE two girls were surprised at Roxy's telephoned invitation, but because they were both unsettled and anxious to get news, and thought perhaps Barney would telephone to Roxy or she might have had a letter, they went. Margaret, mainly because she loved to be where Barney had been, and also because she had known and loved Roxy for years. And Cornelia because she was lonely, just didn't know what to do; and she liked to be with Margaret.

Roxy had told them to come early, but they reached there a little before dinner time, and as they stepped up to the door Barney swung it open, and stood smiling to greet them.

"Oh!" they exclaimed in delight. "You've *come back!* How *grand!* But wouldn't they let you go? *What* has happened?"

A flame of lovely rose swept up into Margaret's cheeks and her eyes shone with delight.

"Welcome!" said Barney joyously, and turned to the other tall soldier just behind him. "And let me introduce my friend Stormy Applegate!" He grabbed Stormy's arm and brought him forward. And then, and not till then, he turned and took his Margaret in his arms and kissed her. Right there before them all, when nobody had been told yet that they belonged to each other. Margaret's cheeks grew flame-color, but she gasped and returned the kiss eagerly, and then hid her face on Barney's shoulder.

But she needn't have minded, for when she at last ventured to peek out from those enfolding arms that held her close and still more closely, she saw that the other two were not looking at her at all, they were just standing there holding hands, both pairs of hands and looking into one another's faces, with a look of great wonder and delight, as if they were getting to know one another all in a minute, in place of the years of acquaintance they wished they might have had. As if no one else were by and they had nothing to think of but one another.

So Margaret relaxed and just stayed there in Barney's arms, that drew her close and then Barney bent his head and kissed her again quite thoroughly.

Suddenly Stormy caught on to what had been happening, and he said in his droll way:

"Oh, is *that* the order of the day? You should have told me. Do you mind, Cornelia? Because you see I've known you for a very long time, even though you may not remember," and quickly he drew her to him and kissed her, almost shyly, if Stormy could do anything shyly—certainly reverently. And then those two were for the moment oblivious to everything but their two selves.

A moment more and a little silver bell tinkled and they looked up to see a puzzled but delighted Roxy standing in the doorway ringing the table bell for attention.

"Children, your dinner is ready," she called. "Would

you like to have it hot or would you prefer to eat it cold?"

Laughingly they drew apart, and the two couples, hand in hand went out to the dining room, where was a table loaded with good things. Hot chicken with dumplings sending forth a savory steam, little new peas and potatoes out of the garden, the first that were ready to eat, crisp lettuce with nuts and apples for salad, crisp celery, and on the sideboard a great glass dish heaped with luscious strawberries, flanked by a pitcher of rich golden cream. *Real* cream from a pampered cow who wouldn't have known what a ration stamp was if she'd been offered one.

"Oh boy!" said Stormy as he held out Cornelia's chair, "gaze on that! And to think that I once was glad to get an ancient raw egg, and cried for more when it was gone!"

Amid the laughter they sat down and Barney bowed his head:

"Lord, our Father, we thank Thee for this food, and we thank Thee most of all that Thou hast answered our prayers and brought our Stormy back to us safely. We thank Thee that Thou art our Savior who hast saved us, all of us, and taught us to know Thee and to love Thee better than anything else in life. We all of us thank Thee today. For Christ's sake, Amen."

Roxy stood by with folded hands and unspeakable joy in her face, her eyes closed and a smile on her lips. She was feeling how glad Barney's mother would be about this.

It was a wonderful dinner, every crumb appreciated, every bit of it eaten, after they had made sure that Roxy had saved enough for Joel and herself. And then they went back into the living room for a few minutes and stood beaming at one another.

"I'll tell you what," said Stormy. "Let's go out and take a walk in the lovely twilight. I want to tell Cornelia something." Cornelia looked up and smiled assent.

"Well," said Barney, "I was just wishing we would because I want to tell a lot of things to Margaret."

So, into the twilight they went, holding hands again, and walking very close to one another.

"We're going to see Margaret's mother first," announced Barney. "We want to show Stormy off to her. She's been praying as hard as any of us for his return."

"Why sure," said Stormy, "I like to be shown off to nice people who've been praying me home again. How about it Cornelia?"

"Oh, of course," said Cornelia. "She's very nice. You'll like her, Stormy."

"Of course I will," said Stormy drolly. "Look who she has for a daughter."

And then amid laughter and joy they started on, Barney and Sunny taking the lead, the other two coming more and more slowly, and talking in low tones.

"I've known you a long time, Cornelia, only you didn't know me."

"Oh yes, I did. My brother has told me so much about you that I feel as if we almost might have grown up together."

Stormy smiled and slipped her hand in his other one, putting the nearest arm about her shoulders.

"But you see, I've been loving you a long long time, too."

"Well," said Cornelia quietly, "maybe it just wasn't very formal of me, but I'm afraid I've almost been loving you too. Of course I haven't any right to be loving you, only Jim told me so much about you, and he adored you so thoroughly that I somehow couldn't help loving everything you did. And I've cherished a little picture of you I stole from my brother. I don't think he knows I have it but I wouldn't give it up for anything."

"Yes?" said Stormy. "But, my dear, I have carried a picture of you close to my heart all through this war. It has helped me a lot over hard places, and it got so thoroughly into my soul that once when I was ill and hungry and burning with fever, I thought it was you who came into the shack where I was lying on a bunch of old potato bags and hay, and laid your cool little hand on my forehead. And I have seen you often when I looked up to the clouds and I thought you were an angel smiling down at me. Sometimes it seemed that if it hadn't been for you I never would have got through to come home. And then after the crash—I know you haven't heard about that yet, but I'm coming to it. After the crash you came alongside and wakened me, when otherwise I would have burned to death. And when I got out at last safely, and there was a long way to walk to safety, you walked with me sometimes in the night, and I held your hand this way. Of course I had no right to let myself think all that out, and dream of you, but I'm asking you for the right now, Cornelia. Will you let me love you? And will you marry me, and be with me always?"

And Cornelia lifted a lovely face and said softly, "Yes, Stormy, darling!"

And a couple of steps ahead came Barney's voice.

"Oh, I say, you two, come up to the surface and look around you. This is where we turn in to the farm, and it's worth seeing. You might not recognize it next time you come this way unless you look around now."

At first they didn't hear at all, but the third time he called they came to themselves with a start, and quickened their steps.

"Yes, it's beautiful, especially in the soft dusk," said

Cornelia. "And you'll just love Margaret's mother, Stormy."

"Well, if I have any love left over from loving you I might try," said Stormy. "Come on, let's go in. Say, isn't that a thrush singing at evening? I haven't heard a thrush sing for years, but I never forget those silver spoons against cut glass they use for accompaniment. Say, isn't that some song?"

They marched into the house with arms about one another.

Barney went calling through the house:

"Where are you, Sunny's mother? Where are you Mother Roselle?" and they could hear her running from upstairs:

"Yes, I'm here, Barney dear. Coming at once!"

"Well we've come to get your blessing for another couple, Mother. That is, I *think* we have? There seemed to be signs that way as we came over. How about it, Stormy? Put it over yet, or am I butting in too soon?"

"You're butting in, Barn, but I guess it's all right with me. How about it Cornelia?"

Cornelia lifted lovely dark eyes and smiled, her face scarlet from all this publicity, but very joyous, and twinkled her consent.

"Okay, company, let's all kneel right here and get that mother-blessing. We'll need it plenty I'm sure as the years go by," said Barney.

It was Stormy who led the way. They came and stood in line before her, and at his slightly lifted hand they all knelt and bowed their heads.

Mother Roselle always knew how to fit right into anything, and she came close to them, pushed their heads close together, and laid one hand on Barney's and Margaret's heads, and the other hand on Cornelia's and Stormy's heads.

"May the dear Lord bless you, my children," she said softly, and then after an instant they arose and each of them kissed her tenderly.

"Now," said Barney, "we're going back to my house and arrange about these weddings. They ought to come off soon you know for we don't know just when we may be called to move on. We don't want a thing like this hanging fire. We've got to decide whether it will be two weddings or one double one. We've got to decide where it will be, and who shall officiate, and what we shall wear. If I'm not mistaken there's a wedding veil somewhere in my house among the heirlooms. I might wear that. Do you all think it would be becoming over my uniform?"

Hortense and her crowd happened to be driving by the Roselle farm just then and they heard peals of laughter coming from the front windows which were open.

"Mercy! What do you suppose they find to laugh about like that in there?" said Hortense.

"Well, if I'm not greatly mistaken I think you'll find that Barney is home, and he's probably down there."

"Yes," said Amelia in a kind of triumphant voice, "I saw him arrive, and he had the best-looking soldier with him, even a little taller than Barney, and just stunningly handsome. He's probably there. I saw Sunny go down and get that Cornelia girl just before dinner time. They're probably all there!"

"Oh!" said Hortense, and was very quiet for the rest of the evening.

But in the old white farmhouse there was much joy. Sunny's mother looked up with a smile.

"You would all be very welcome to have the weddings here of course," she said with a smile.

"And I know my aunt would say that too, of course,"

said Cornelia, "and perhaps feel hurt if I went somewhere else."

"You better come to my house," said Barney. "After all, I'm the one who started all these weddings."

Sunny gave him a radiant smile, but then she spoke in a quiet voice:

"I think that I would like to be married in the church," she said. "Then we could feel that Barney's mother was there, sitting right in the middle of the church in the same pew where she sat ever since she was married."

The look that Barney gave her then was one she would remember always, and so would the others.

"I think that would be nice," said Cornelia, "then nobody could be hurt. And it certainly would be nice to have the two weddings together. Barney and Stormy have always been so much to one another. How I wish my brother Jim could be here."

"Of course," said Stormy, "I'll see if we can't arrange for that. How about it Barn? Don't you suppose we can do that over the phone or would we have to go down to Washington to have it fixed?" He was grinning, but the two young men gave a twinkling promise to one another of what they were going to try to do.

"Well, it will be great to have some uniforms anyway," said Cornelia. "And if it is in a church you can just invite anybody who wants to come, and not have to bother about invitations. You couldn't get them engraved now, very likely anyway, not if we have it in a hurry."

"And about what we'll wear," said Margaret, looking toward her mother, "would your wedding dress be all right?"

"Why of course," said her mother. "I've always kept

it for you and it fits you nicely. People are not getting a lot of new finery these wartimes."

"Well, I can wear my mother's wedding dress. It's in storage, but I can have it sent at once. And the veils. Shall we wear veils?"

"Yes," said Mrs. Roselle. "Veils are always lovely to remember. I think mine is still good. It has some real lace on it. Of course it will be somewhat yellow, but that will make it all the more worth-while."

"Why, this is great," said Cornelia, "getting a wedding all arranged in a few minutes like this. But then that is the way everything has to be done in wartimes, and after all, when the war is over we may learn not to spend so much time on trifles and nonsense. But I think this is going to be pretty, too. There'll be a few friends we'll want to ask down. There's a hotel not too far away for them to come to, isn't there? And as for a reception we can just stand at the back of the church after the cere-mony and shake hands."

"Great!" said Sunny. "I was afraid you would want a big reception."

"Not on your life!" said Stormy with a sigh of relief.

"Here neither," said Barney with satisfaction. "But I just want to state here and now that I think Stormy and I have found the two best girls on all the face of the earth. They've settled their weddings without a squabble, and they care more about their Lord, and their men than they do about style or what the world thinks. Come on now and let's go home and think it over. There's another day coming, and Storm, you and I have a few things to arrange. When did they say we had to come down to Washington and be decorated? I'd like to have that over so I could wear my decorations at the wedding, for I don't much think I'll flaunt them any other time, except to show them to my grandchildren. Come on now, let's go down and tell Auntie Kimberly and see how she likes it, and then everybody's happy from now on."

So they presently took up their march down the road, and the gang of pleasure-seekers came driving glumly down behind them and passed them.

"There they are," said Janet Harper.

"Heavens! Isn't he tall," said Hortense. "But they didn't speak. I don't think that was very nice of them."

"They didn't even see us," said Amelia. "They didn't see anybody but each other. They were holding hands."

"I thought your pattern Barney never did things like that," said Janet Harper.

"Oh, shut up, can't you, Janet, I have a terrible headache!" said Hortense.

But it presently got around that the wedding was coming off soon, and everybody in town who wanted to come was invited.

"I don't suppose they knew any better than to think that is good form," said Hortense with her nose in the air. But she arranged to buy a new dress to wear to the wedding to dazzle that New York girl.

Barney and Stormy were called to Washington to receive their decorations and to speak over the radio just three days before the day they had set for the wedding. And the girls arranged to go along. The whole thing was on the radio of course, and the gang at home furtively and jealously listened to it.

And then the day of the weddings came, and in the morning Jim Mayberry arrived!

It appeared that the two bridegrooms had arranged the whole matter with their superior officers, and Jim was back from his mission and due for a furlough anyway. So he came in a plane, and Jim was to be best man for both of his old buddies.

And there were other uniforms in the audience besides

those three. A lot of the old friends and fellow-soldiers from the army, a few sailors. Even the admiral came with a few of his fellow-officers who wanted to do honor to the young men who had served so wonderfully in the service.

It was both the young minister and the old one who had the service together, and the whole plan of it had been carefully arranged so that the service would be a testimony to the world, of how Christ could save from sin, what true marriage should be, and how a Christian home should be carried on. It was only a few words, bits of Bible quotations, that carried these great lessons, but they were there, and the gang in the back seat stopped whispering and listened, and more than one besides Amelia Haskell said, "Heavens! If I thought I could have a marriage like that it would be worth-while trying to be a Christian, and find a fellow who believed such things."

As they came out from the church, the sun was beginning to set, and the birds were singing their evening songs. Wood thrushes spilling out their silver notes, a lot of other birds.

"I'm glad they are singing," said Margaret.

"Yes," said Cornelia as she paused by the car and looked up to the trees by the church, "Isn't it wonderful?"

"Yes," said Barney solemnly, a beautiful light in his face, "The Time of the Singing of Birds is come."

About the Author

Grace Livingston Hill is well-known as one of the most prolific writers of romantic fiction. Her personal life was fraught with joys and sorrows not unlike those experienced by many of her fictional heroines.

Born in Wellsville, New York, Grace nearly died during the first hours of life. But her loving parents and friends turned to God in prayer. She survived miraculously, thus her thankful father named her Grace.

Grace was always close to her father, a Presbyterian minister, and her mother, a published writer. It was from them that she learned the art of storytelling. When Grace was twelve, a close aunt surprised her with a hardbound, illustrated copy of one of Grace's stories. This was the beginning of Grace's journey into being a published author.

In 1892 Grace married Fred Hill, a young minister, and they soon had two lovely young daughters. Then came 1901, a difficult year for Grace—the year when, within months of each other, both her father and husband died.

Suddenly Grace had to find a new place to live (her home was owned by the church where her husband had been pastor). It was a struggle for Grace to raise her young daughters alone, but through everything she kept writing. In 1902 she produced *The Angel of His Presence, The Story of a Whim,* and *An Unwilling Guest.* In 1903 her two books *According to the Pattern* and *Because of Stephen* were published.

It wasn't long before Grace was a well-known author, but she wanted to go beyond just entertaining her readers. She soon included the message of God's salvation through Jesus Christ in each of her books. For Grace, the most important thing she did was not write books but share the message of salvation, a message she felt God wanted her to share through the abilities he had given her.

In all, Grace Livingston Hill wrote more than one hundred books, all of which have sold thousands of copies and have touched the lives of readers around the world with their message of "enduring love" and the true way to lasting happiness: a relationship with God through his Son, Jesus Christ.

In an interview shortly before her death, Grace's devotion to her Lord still shone clear. She commented that whatever she had accomplished had been God's doing. She was only his servant, one who had tried to follow his teaching in all her thoughts and writing.

Don't miss these Grace Livingston Hill romance novels!

Mail your order with check or money order for the price of the book plus $2.00 for postage and handling to: **Tyndale Family Products, P.O. Box 448, Wheaton, IL 60189-0448.** Allow 4-6 weeks for delivery. Prices subject to change.

The Grace Livingston Hill romance novels are available at your local book-store, or you may order by mail (U.S. and territories only). For your conve-nience, use this page to place your order or write the information on a separate sheet of paper, including the order number for each book.